To Mike
and Mary

Happy Christmas
2004
and

Happy Gardening

from

Nanette & Bryan

THE GARDENER'S COMPANION

Edited by Vicky Bamforth

A THINK BOOK FOR

ROBSON BOOKS

OTHER BOOKS IN THE COMPANION SERIES

The Cook's Companion
Edited by Jo Swinnerton
ISBN-1-86105-772-5

The Wildlife Companion
Edited by Malcolm Tait and Olive Tayler
ISBN 1-86105-770-9

The Traveller's Companion
Edited by Georgina Newbery and Rhiannon Guy
ISBN 1-86105-773-3

SERIES EDITORS

Malcolm Tait and Emma Jones

Old gardeners never die...
they only go to seed.

Anon

THINK
A Think Book
for Robson Books

First published in Great Britain in 2004 by
Robson Books
The Chrysalis Building, Bramley Road, London W10 6SP

An imprint of **Chrysalis** Books Group plc

Text © Think Publishing 2004
Design and layout © Think Publishing 2004
The moral rights of the author have been asserted

Edited by Vicky Bamforth
The Companion team: Sarah Bove, James Collins, Harry Glass,
Rhiannon Guy, Annabel Holmes, Emma Jones,
Lou Millward Tait and Malcolm Tait

Think Publishing
The Pall Mall Deposit
124-128 Barlby Road, London W10 6BL
www.thinkpublishing.co.uk

ISBN 1-86105-771-7

Printed and bound by Clays Ltd, Bungay, Suffolk NR35 1ED
The publishers and authors have made every effort to ensure the accuracy and
currency of the information in The Gardener's Companion. Similarly, every
effort has been made to contact copyright holders. We apologise for any
unintentional errors or omissions. The publisher and authors disclaim any
liability, loss, injury or damage incurred as a consequence, directly or
indirectly, of the use and application of the contents of this book.

More than anything,
I must have flowers always, always.

Claude Monet, artist

A GREEN AND FRUITY THANK YOU

This book would not have been possible without the research, ideas, and dogged support of:

Caro, John and Rosemary Bamforth, Janice Bhend, Jo Bourne, Yeh Htoo, Nigel and Pamela Ince, Katherine Lawrey, Clemmie Perowne, Nick Smith and Verity Wilcox.

Special thanks also to the librarians at the Royal Horticultural Society's Linley Library for their knowledge, helpfulness and kind words.

INTRODUCTION

The Gardener's Companion is not a guide to gardening, nor is it a list of famous gardens to visit. It does not tell you how to lay decking or put down a pond liner, nor will it answer gardening questions such as how to handle a heliconia or prune a pear tree. In fact this book will tell you nothing about gardening at all.

But whatever you garden; whether it's a country vegetable plot or a small city terrace, *The Gardener's Companion* will have something for you. This is the book you will want for the moments you throw down your weeding fork with relief and settle into a hammock under the shade of an old tree.

Packed within these pages are the real burning garden facts that you always wanted to know, but never knew where to find. Who grew the first Cox's Orange Pippin tree? What is Saffron Walden famous for? What happened when David Niven found Greta Garbo swimming naked in a pool? Who is the patron saint of lost gardening tools? And where did the practice of kissing under the mistletoe come from?

The Gardener's Companion is the only gardening book that will tell you the answers to all these essential need-to-know gardening questions, and what's more, it should inspire a few laughs along the way.

Vicky Bamforth, Editor

BLOOMING GOOD IDEAS

George Acland was the first person to commercially manufacture jute garden twine, in Dundee, Scotland in 1828.

French aristocrat Bertrand de Moleville invented secateurs in 1818 for trimming in orchards, vineyards and rose gardens.

Carly Nyberg invented the flame weeder in 1881. No longer the most popular form of weeding, the flame weeder has found fame elsewhere as a blowtorch for welding metal, a wartime flame-thrower and more recently, a fail-safe method of creating the sugary crust on a crème brulée.

Fourth century AD Chinese civil servant and poet, Ton Guen-ming is thought to have dreamt up the idea of the Chinese penjing (tray garden). Penjing is the predecessor to bonsai growing, which itself widely thought of as Japanese, was brought to Japan from China by Buddhist monks in 1195 AD.

The well-known Greek philosopher and writer, Theophrastus was also a top naturalist and gardening guru. He was the first to systematically classify plants (beating the more well-known Linnaeus by a few centuries), the first to classify roses and the first to establish what some consider the world's first botanic garden at the Lyceum in 300 BC.

In 1964, the archdeacon of Winchester Cathedral Robert Sharrack devised the simplest mole trap to date – a pot in the ground.

In 1640, Leonard Mascall was the first to describe in print his effective method for slug control. It essentially involved picking them up by hand.

Jan van der Heide invented the standard leather garden hose in 1672. Not until the mid-19th century was it updated. British chemist, Henry Bewley was the first to manufacture garden hoses out of gutta percha (a natural material similar to rubber from Malaysia). In the mid-20th century, gutta percha was also used to cover transatlantic cables, which just goes to prove that all the best things come out of the garden.

ORANGES ARE NOT THE ONLY FRUIT

The world record for the largest number of different fruits produced from the same tree is five: apricot, cherry, nectarine, plum, and peach. The fruit species were grafted on to root stock in 2000 by Luis H Carrasco of Chile.

10 *Area, in millions of hectares, of rainforest destroyed by fire in Indonesia in 1997*

ARTIFICIAL FLOWERS

Word for 'flower'	Language	Spoken in
Loote	Quenya	Middle Earth
Seregon	Sindarin	Middle Earth
Loth	Silmarillion	Middle Earth
Lagga	Romulan	Star Trek

LATHER BLATHER

Saponin is the chemical responsible for producing the frothy lather in soap. Plants that contain saponin include:

• Soapwort, a European herbaceous perennial whose leaves produce a green lather when rubbed or boiled in water.

• *Balinites aegyptiaca*, a spiny tree that grows in Sudan and Chad, and was used in ancient Egypt. It contains an edible oil, which also makes a foaming soap.

• The soap tree, which originated in Chile. Its bark is used as both a soap and a foaming agent for drinks.

• The lac tree. Oil from its seeds is used as a hair oil. It was a popular remedy for gentlemen during the Victorian times, when it was known as Madagascar oil.

THE RAKE'S PROGRESS

Being an experienced gardener Gilbert knew how to duck the flying rake. Oswald, sadly, was new to the game.

The Greek philosopher Socrates died in 399 BC in Athens after being forced to drink the poison colchicines, which is derived from the spotted hemlock plant, which grows near rivers, streams, hedges and some gardens in Britain. Socrates had been condemned to death after a state-sponsored trial, which found him guilty of impiety, heresy and corrupting the youth of Athens. His trial, stubborn defence and painful death were witnessed by friends and written up by Plato:

Then holding the cup to his lips, quite readily and cheerfully he drank off the poison. And hitherto most of us had been able to control our sorrow; but now when we saw him drinking, and saw too that he had finished the draught, we could no longer forbear, and in spite of myself my own tears were flowing fast; so that I covered my face and wept over myself, for certainly I was not weeping over him, but at the thought of my own calamity in having lost such a companion. Nor was I the first, for Crito, when he found himself unable to restrain his tears, had got up and moved away, and I followed; and at that moment, Apollodorus, who had been weeping all the time, broke out into a loud cry which made cowards of us all. Socrates alone retained his calmness: What is this strange outcry? he said. I sent away the women mainly in order that they might not offend in this way, for I have heard that a man should die in peace. Be quiet, then, and have patience. When we heard that, we were ashamed, and refrained our tears; and he walked about until, as he said, his legs began to fail, and then he lay on his back, according to the directions, and the man who gave him the poison now and then looked at his feet and legs; and after a while he pressed his foot hard and asked him if he could feel; and he said, no; and then his leg, and so upwards and upwards, and showed us that he was cold and stiff. And he felt them himself, and said: When the poison reaches the heart, that will be the end. He was beginning to grow cold about the groin, when he uncovered his face, for he had covered himself up, and said (they were his last words) – he said: Crito, I owe a cock to Asclepius; will you remember to pay the debt? The debt shall be paid, said Crito; is there anything else? There was no answer to this question; but in a minute or two a movement was heard, and the attendants uncovered him; his eyes were set, and Crito closed his eyes and mouth. Such was the end, Echecrates, of our friend, whom I may truly call the wisest, and justest, and best of all the men whom I have ever known.

The death of Socrates from Plato's *Phaedo*, translated by Benjamin Jowett

A GARDENER'S RAIN CHECK

Luke Howard is known by weather forecasters as the father of meteorology. An untrained scientist, Howard was an amateur meteorologist who, while travelling daily between his home in Plaistow and his office in London, observed different types of clouds in the sky. From his notes, he devised a straightforward naming system (in Latin of course) and in December 1802, published a paper with his descriptions, which caused a sensation among scientists.

Prior to Howard's classification, clouds were simply described as: dark, white, woolly, buttermilk, mare's tails, or mackerel skies, hence the rhymes: 'Mackerel sky, mackerel sky, never long wet, never long dry' and 'Mare's tails and mackerel scales make lofty ships take in their sails'.

The 10 fundamental cloud definitions originating from Howard's classification in Latin with their original translation are:

Cloud Type	Symbol	Translation	Height of base
Cirrus	Ci	wispy clouds	17,000-35,000ft
Cirrocumulus	Cc	a wispy lump of clouds	17,000-35,000ft
Cirrostratus	Cs	a wispy layer of clouds	17,000-35,000ft
Altocumulus	Ac	a middle lump of clouds	7,000-17,000ft
Altostratus	As	a middle layer of clouds	8,000-17,000ft
Nimbostratus	Ns	a low layer of rain clouds	8,000-17,000ft
Cumulus	Cu	lumpy clouds	1,200-6,000ft
Cumulonimbus	Cb	big lumpy clouds with rain	1,000-5,000ft
Stratocumulus	Sc	a layer of lumpy clouds	1,200-7,000ft
Stratus	St	a low layer of lumpy clouds	surface-1,500ft

ON THE GRAPEVINE

A single flow'r he sent me, since we met.
All tenderly his messenger he chose;
Deep-hearted, pure, with scented dew still wet –
One perfect rose.

I knew the language of the floweret;
'My fragile leaves', it said, 'his heart enclose'
Love long has taken for his amulet
One perfect rose.

Why is it no one ever sent me yet
One perfect limousine, do you suppose?
Ah no, it's always just my luck to get
One perfect rose.

Dorothy Parker, *One Perfect Rose*

Country gentlemen may find, that in using my machine themselves, an amusing, useful and healthy exercise.
EDWARD BEARD BUDDING, inventor of the lawnmower

GARDENS IN HISTORY

In September 1651, Charles II is said to have taken refuge in an oak tree in the estate of Boscobel House following his defeat at the hands of Oliver Cromwell at the Battle of Worcester. The tree, which became known as the 'Royal Oak' or the 'King Charles II Oak' is probably the most famous of its kind in England, and there are a number of stories, many of them inaccurate, about poor Charles's night under the leaves.

Local records, however, do refer to the oak tree, and suggest that Charles did indeed sit under it in discussion with royalist officer Colonel Careless while he spent his nights hidden in Boscobel House. According to the legend, the King climbed into the oak – a large tree, covered with ivy – when it was judged too unsafe for him to remain in the house. He spent a night concealed in its branches, while food was apparently sent up with a nut hook.

Years later the tree was enclosed with iron railings and a sign put up testifying to its important role in royal history. However, when the tree was examined in 1974, it was pronounced no older than 250 years, dating its origin to 1724, 73 years after King Charles II apparently climbed into its mature branches. The tree's ageing throws doubt on historical records, and the existence of the Royal Oak remains a mystery.

BACKING THE WRONG NORSE

When a family started digging up their garden in Fife, they came across some huge slabs hidden in the ground. Believing they had found an old Norse settlement, they excitedly called in the council who sent in their archaeologists to investigate. But after six months of minute excavations when tiny amounts of soil were carefully lifted and dusted away, the archaeologists discovered all they were unearthing was a 40-year-old garden patio.

Admitting they had mistakenly ignored evidence of a child's gas mask, the red-faced archaeologists promised they would be more careful next time.

Although allotments are a relatively modern invention, the idea of shared plots of land go far back in British history to about 1000 AD when Saxon fields were cleared by communities and shared out. But this communal pattern of landholding came under threat as more land fell into the hands of the Crown and the Church.

During the reign of Henry VIII, land was taken away from the Church and given to individual members of the court, with the first enclosure of common land for noble landowners taking place during the reign of Elizabeth I. Enclosure of common land continued throughout the 17th and 18th centuries and reached a peak during the 19th century when so much land was enclosed that the government feared a wide scale revolt from landless rural peasants who could no longer scour the common areas of the countryside in search of food.

Years of protest ultimately led to the 1908 *Smallholdings and Allotments Act*, which required local councils to provide land for the creation of allotments. And this Act still defines the plots' standard size measurements: 10 rods (about 250 square metres).

Allotments saw another huge spurt of growth during both world wars, when the number of allotments increased to about 1,500,000. In World War II, for example, it is estimated that food production from allotments totalled an impressive 1,300,000 tonnes – almost a tonne of food per plot.

Over the last 50 years, interest in allotments has tailed off as we increasingly buy our fruit and vegetables from supermarkets. The number of allotments in use today – less than 250,000 – is less than half the number used in 1969. But food scares, worries about GM crops and organic farming are starting to turn allotments around.

In 1992, allotments received a national boost when Britain signed up to *Agenda 21*, the international agreement that compels signatories to make efforts to promote the environment. As a result many local councils are again promoting the allotment idea. Despite the positive benefits of allotments, they are still threatened by building developers. If your allotment is under threat, visit www.allotments-uk.com to find out about other battles taking place up and down the country.

If you haven't got a green space of your own, consider renting an allotment – the annual cost can be as little as £15 to £20, and you can get fit, eat healthily and make new friends too. For more information on how to rent an allotment, contact the National Society of Allotment and Leisure Gardeners at www.nsalg.demon.co.uk.

BUSH WHACKED

According to a report in the *Sunday Mirror*, President Bush's 2003 visit to Buckingham Palace resulted in the Queen's gardens being damaged – to the tune of thousands of pounds. The paper gleefully reported that perfectly manicured lawns were turned into helipads, exotic plants were trampled by keen security service agents and the Queen's personal flock of flamingos were so traumatised (was it at the sight of the President?) that they may never return to their favoured spot in the garden again.

BLOOMING PUZZLES

Homophones are words that sound the same but have different meanings. Find two homophones in the following sentence:
A waterless vegetable
Answer on page 153

ON THE GRAPEVINE

I dug
I levelled
I weeded
I seeded
I planted
I waited
I weeded
I pleaded
I mulched
I gulched
I watered
I waited
I fumbled
I grumbled
I poked
I hoped

so GROW... Dammit
Diana Anthony, *A Sense of Humus*

WHAT A GREAT VIEW

The word gazebo comes from the Victorian expression 'gaze-about', a shelter from where you can see your entire garden.

QUOTE UNQUOTE

*I once heard it said that rich people used to show their wealth by
the size of their bedding-plant list: 10,000 plants for a squire;
20,000 for a baronet; 30,000 for an earl; and 50,000 for a duke.*
ERNEST FIELD, gardener, gives an insight into
gardening in the days before sports cars

IN SOCIETY

Society	Date founded
Royal Horticultural Society	1804
National Chrysanthemum Society	1846
Royal National Rose Society	1876
British Pteridological Society	1891
Daffodil Society	1898
National Viola and Pansy Society	1911
British Iris Society	1922
British Gladiolus Society	1926
Herb Society	1927
Delphinium Society	1928
Alpine Garden Society	1929
National Begonia Society	1948
British National Carnation Society	1949
British Pelargonium and Geranium Society	1951
Orchid Society of Great Britain	1951
Henry Doubleday Research Association	1954
Hardy Plant Society	1957
National Association of Flower Arrangement Societies	1959
National Vegetable Society	1960
Heather Society	1963
British Hosta and Hemerocallis Society	1981

GNOME GNOTES

Anyone who considers gnomes tacky and cheap should take note – in
1997, a garden gnome, believed to be the oldest in the world, was
insured for one million pounds. The gnome, known as Lampy, is the
sole survivor of a set of 21 gnomes imported to Britain in the 1840s
by early gnome fanatic, Sir Charles Isham. Sir Charles' daughters
were not, however, fond of the gaudy little workers and had the set
removed. Lampy escaped his rubbish bin destiny by a stroke of good
fortune and remained hiding in the long grass.

GARDENS IN THE SKY

If you live in a city, don't have a garden, but can access a roof space, why not turn it into a garden? Not only is it perfect for growing small flavour-bursting produce like tomatoes, but if you get planning permission, it can add value to the property and provide a space for you to relax in the sun. There are strong environmental benefits too:

In cities, very little land is not paved – over 75% of most cities are covered with asphalt, and this produces 'heat islands', which make cities up to 8°F hotter than surrounding rural areas. When air temperatures are high, roof surface temperatures can be almost twice as hot. Plants transform heat and soil moisture into humidity and cool the air. By increasing the number of green plants in a city, temperatures will actually fall.

Roof gardens also insulate houses better in the winter (on average, a flat roof well-stocked with plants can provide 25% more insulation), and a roof garden can minimise heat loss due to wind speeds by as much as 50%.

A roof garden can also improve our quality of water. When rain falls on a forest or meadow, about 40% evaporates and returns to the atmosphere, 30% reaches shallow aquifers that feed plants, and the remaining 30% flows into the water table. But in a city, only 15% evaporates and just 5% reaches the water table. The remaining 75% becomes surface run-off which runs into storm-water drains that collect the water and deposit it into rivers and lakes (causing a decline in water quality). A roof garden can reduce this percentage to 25% by drawing the water to its plants.

And best of all, roof gardens can provide space for animals and birds who have suffered habitat loss through development.

In Greater London, rooftops account for an astonishing 24,000ha. And English Nature believes that, throughout the UK, an estimated 20,000ha of urban roofs could be vegetated with little or no structural alterations.

THE FIRST GARDENING TOOLS

The first gardening tools were believed to have been constructed about 40,000 years ago from animal bones. Mattocks were made from sheep's horns, tied to sticks; dibbers were constructed out of mammoth's ribs; and shovels were made from the shoulder blades of oxen.

NECTAR OF THE GODS

Plants inspired by deities of the classical world

Name	Namesake
Achillea	Achilles, the famed warrior who was slain by an arrow shot into his heel
Amaryllis	a countrywoman referred to by Virgil
Artemisia	the virgin goddess of hunting
Cassiope	Andromeda's mother
Gentiana	Gentius, King of Illyria
Hebe	Jupiter's daughter and Hercules' wife
Helenium	Helen of Troy
Iris	the goddess of the rainbow
Nerine	Daughter of Nereus and a sea nymph
Paeonia	the god of healing

BLOOMING PUZZLES

Spot the real feline:
Hairy cat's ear • Cat's whisker
Pussy toes • Cat's tongue • Cat's teeth
Answer on page 153

ON THE GRAPEVINE

Soon will the high Midsummer pomps come on,
Soon will the musk carnations break and swell,
Soon shall we have gold-dusted snapdragon,
Sweet-William with his homely cottage-smell,
And stocks in fragrant blow;
Roses that down the alleys shine afar,
And open, jasmine-muffled lattices,
And groups under the dreaming garden-trees,
And the full moon, and the white evening-star.
**Matthew Arnold, *Thyrsis: A Monody, to Commemorate
the Author's Friend, Arthur Hugh Clough***

QUOTE UNQUOTE

*To be overcome by the fragrance of flowers is a delectable
form of defeat.*
BEVERLEY NICHOLS, author

LOVE IN THE GARDEN

Star-crossed lovers Pyramus and Thisbe met their sad fate as a result of parental disapproval in the city of Babylon. Although the neighbouring families disallowed the union, the young lovers contrived in secret to meet through a hole in the garden wall. But one day, on the way to the reunion, Thisbe happened upon a lion, which seized and tore some clothes she had dropped in her haste to escape. Pyramus, on finding the clothes, assumed Thisbe had been killed, and stabbed himself to death, and she in return, killed herself with his sword, on discovery of his body.

Shakespeare made the tale famous by including it in *A Midsummer Night's Dream*, but the tale did not originate with him, for Ovid – the Roman poet who died in 17 AD – included the tale in his *Metamorphoses, Book 4*. Not that the tale originated with him either; he appears to have heard it from the Greeks and they in turn from the Babylonians.

NOT FOR EATING

Adding flowers to salads is quite colourful and very fashionable, with pansies, squash blossoms and daylilies appearing on many restaurant menus. But before you decide to dip the contents of your garden in the Hellmann's, make sure they are edible. The following common garden flowers are not:

Plant	Poison
Almond blossom	hydrocyanic acid
Amaryllis	hippeastrine, lycorine and amaryllidine
Autumn crocus	colchicine
Christmas rose	glycoside hellebrin
Daffodil	galanthamine, haemanthamine, lycorine
Delphinium	delphinine and ajacine
Flax	linamarin
Glory lily	cochicine, superbine and lumicolchicine
Heliotrope	pyrrolozidine
Horse chestnut	aesculin
Hydrangea	hydrangin
Japanese honeysuckle	saponin, tannin and inositol
Lily-of-the-valley	convallatoxin
Morning glory	lysergic acid and isoergine
Rhododendron	grayanotoxin and andromedotoxin
Rue	furocoumarins and rutin
Star-of-Bethlehem	convallatoxin convalliside
Sweet pea	aliphatic amino acid glycoside
Wisteria	wisterin

EARTHWORMITIS?

Earthworms have become critical creatures in the study of science and many scientists refer to them as 'keystone organisms'. Not only widely admired in the garden, where they function as early warning systems in deteriorating natural environments, they are also useful in assessing toxicity levels of new chemicals. And, although to look at them you wouldn't think so, their bodies are similar to humans with centralised nervous systems, blood vessels, haemoglobin, urine-producing tubes similar to kidneys, a liver-like tissue and an ability to repair their own wounds. It's not surprising then to find earthworms in laboratories all over the world. They are used to study subjects such as ageing, blood disorders and inflammatory diseases, like rheumatoid arthritis.

GARDENS OF HISTORY

In the grounds of Holwood House, is a stone seat where William Pitt the Younger was accustomed to sitting and discussing political issues with fellow MPs when he was Prime Minister in the 1780s. Indeed, it was on this bench that Tory MP and anti-slave trade campaigner William Wilberforce announced to Pitt his resolve to bring an end to the slave trade. Overlooking the seat was a grand old oak tree that subsequently became known as the Wilberforce Oak, in memory of Wilberforce's convictions. Sadly the original oak has succumbed to old age, but in 1952, an oak sapling was planted among the remains of the old tree in continual recognition of Wilberforce's achievement.

QUOTE UNQUOTE

To forget how to dig the earth and to tend the soil is to forget ourselves.
MAHATMA GANDHI

FANTASY GARDENS

In the 1890s, Count Eusebi Guell commissioned Antoni Gaudi to design a garden city on a hill overlooking the city of Barcelona. Gaudi built a collection of mosaic-decorated structures and buildings, including houses that looked like fantasy gingerbread cottages with chimneys in the shape of mushrooms, fountains that emerged from lizards and rough earthy walls inspired by pineapple trees. Park Guell was completed in 1922 and attracts visitors from all over the globe.

Mint's origins in Europe can be traced all the back way to Greek mythology. This wonderfully fragrant herb is named after Minthe, a nymph who won the affections of Pluto, a mighty God and coincidentally a mighty philanderer. To prevent his wife's revenge, he transformed Minthe into a herb.

Mint's historical uses are countless; its health benefits undeniable. Hebrews laid it on synagogue floors for disguising unpleasant smells. Romans flavoured their wines and sauces with it. Mixed with honey into a refreshing paste, it was used by ladies to mask secret wine-sipping, a crime charged with the death penalty in ancient Rome.

Mint can reduce flatulence, cure colds, unblock noses, prevent stomach ulcers, kill bacteria and reduce herpes. To grow this magical herb in your back garden, simply pick your favourite out of 600 varieties, and make sure its roots are contained within a pot, as both roots and aroma tend to take over the garden!

Variegated apple mint
Furry bright green leaves with an apple-menthol fragrance

Banana mint
An exquisite banana flavour; perfect for flavouring ice cream and biscuits

Basil mint
A peppermint base with a spicy tang that is excellent in stews

Chocolate mint
Rich and chocolatey, yet cooling; use it to add flavour to ice cream

Corsican mint
Tiny leaves and a spreading habitat – an alternative to grass

Curly spearmint
Less distinctive, but very good as a marinade for roast lamb

Eau de cologne mint
A citrus scented mint with dark foliage; good in a hot bath

Grapefruit mint
A spearmint flavour with surprising overtones of grapefruit

Variegated ginger mint
A distinctive ginger flavour perfect for fruit salads

Kentucky Colonial mint
A very sweet mint that was carried round the world by Spanish explorers

Orange mint
A smaller-leafed mint with a hint of citrus; often used in perfumes

Peppermint
Strong and cool; use a little in sweet dishes, such as cakes

Variegated pineapple mint
A furry mint with a mild flavour; good for salads

IS THERE A BODY UNDER THE PATIO?

People have the legal right to bury loved ones in the garden under the *Burial Laws Amendment Act* 1880, providing the circumstances of the death are known, a lawful certificate of the cause of death exists and the death has been registered.

Local authority consent is required. A body comes within the definition of 'clinical waste' and it is a criminal offense to dispose of a body except under the provisions of the *Control of Pollution Act* 1974 and the *Environment Protection Act* 1990. A licensed operator is usually needed, but the requirement may be waived in special circumstances. But before you consider burying Auntie Maud beneath the cabbages, spare a thought on how it might affect the value of your property! Ashes can be freely scattered in the garden or buried in a container.

A pet owner can bury their pet in the garden where the pet lived, as long as it is not included within the definition of hazardous waste.

ON THE GRAPEVINE

Some insects feed on rosebuds,
Others feed on carrion,
Between them they devour the earth,
Bugs are totalitarian.

Ogden Nash, *Bugs*

DIRTY STOP OUTS

Why do some flowers only open at night? Nocturnal flowers are generally pollinated by night-time animals and insects, such as moths. The flowers are generally heavily-scented, and often mimic the scents of the female animal that pollinates them. But, although these night-scented garden stocks may have a reputation for being unattractive and spindly plants that dislike intense day-time heat, if you plant them in between other more beautiful flowering plants, they will provide some very rewarding evenings.

Night scented flowers to plant include:

Nottingham catchfly • Night-scented catchfly • Bladder campion

Matthiola bicornis • Sweet rocket • Evening primrose

Nicotiana affinis • Soapwort

European honeysuckle • Italian honeysuckle • Japanese honeysuckle

White jasmine • Dogrose • Sweet briar • Field rose

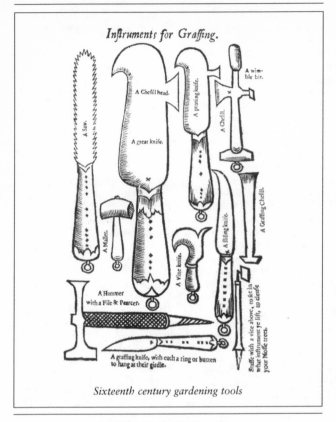

Instruments for Graffing.

A Saw.

A Chefill head.

A pruning knife.

A wimble bit.

A great knife.

A Chefill.

A Maller.

A Vine knife.

A Graffing Chefill.

A flicing knife.

A Hammer with a File & Pearcer.

A graffing knife, with each a ring or button to hang at their girdle.

Staffe with a vice above, to fet in what inftrument ye lift, to dreffe your Mofie trees.

Sixteenth century gardening tools

FAMOUS GARDENERS

Giuseppe Verdi (1813-1901), composer of such beautiful operas as *Rigoletto* and *La Traviata* was also a gentleman farmer and an accomplished gardener. Every time he completed an opera, he would celebrate by planting a tree in his extensive gardens at Santa Agata, Italy. In fact, Verdi almost gave up opera for gardening in 1859. Fortunately, for opera lovers, after only three years of gardening, hunting and fishing on his 10-acre estate, Verdi became bored and returned to the theatre, to write amongst others, the opera masterpieces *Aida*, *Otello* and *Falstaff*.

24 *Weight, in pounds, that a white parasite flower can grow to, in the forests of South-east Asia*

Several years ago, when I was doing much too much television and as a result was more of an objet, if not *d'art, de notorieté* than I am now, Messrs Blackmore and Langdon of Bath, probably the world's leading begonia cultivators – wrote to me saying that each year they introduced three new varieties of begonias, and would I agree to having one of that year's trio named after me? Well, of course, I was thrilled; it put me, after all, on a par with Ena Harkness, black spot or no black spot. Either Mr Blackmore or Mr Langdon (they are to begonias what Mr Steptoe and his associate are to test-tube babies; and obviously charming characters, exuding old-world courtesy) wrote again saying that of the current year's threesome one was a delicate pale lemon with picotée edging, which they didn't feel was really me; the second was a pure white single bloom with faint blush pink centre, which again they didn't feel was me; but the third was a hardy, outsize, long-flowering brilliant scarlet which both Mr B and Mr L felt was me to a T. So I appeared in the catalogue, at £3.75 a tuber, no less. (I came down pretty swiftly to

£2.50 and was last heard of as a sort of remainder job lot at 50p each, or £4.25 for ten of me, p and p extra, but inclusive of VAT.) They even sent me a dozen of myself with the compliments of the management; I still have them, and it's quite something to be able to admire yourself without being accused of narcissism. Begoniaism, perhaps.

But… not so long ago a friend of mine… bought a property in the purlieus of NW1 and found himself for the first time in his life the owner of a fair-sized garden… What better house-warming present, I thought, than a dozen of me? So again I wrote to those charming gentlemen in Bath, and got this back:

We are in receipt of your letter of the 17th inst., with enclosed cheque which we are returning herewith. We find this extremely embarrassing, but it is with very great regret that we have to inform you that you have proved completely infertile and of no use at all for breeding purposes. You have therefore been removed from our catalogue and are no longer available.

Alan Melville,
Gnomes and Gardens

POISONOUS PLANTS

Hollywood actor Steve McQueen was dying from cancer when he decided to opt for a treatment in Mexico that involved the administration of a peach stone enema. Ironically some medical experts believe that this treatment may have hastened his death. Peach stones contain cyanide – as do cherry stones and almonds.

BLOOMING PUZZLES

What do *Pentas Lanceolata*, *Ipomoea alba* and
Helianthus annuus have in common?
Answer on page 153

ON THE GRAPEVINE

I admit that Versailles, Courances and Villandry are superb
achievements of the architectural school of gardening. Yet a garden is
intended for the pleasure of its owner and not for ostentation. Nobody
could sit with his family on the parterre of Versailles and read the
Sunday papers while sipping China tea. Nobody who really cares for
flowers can really want them arranged in patterns as if they were
carpets from Shiraz or Isfahan. Most civilised people prefer the shade
of some dear family tree to the opulence of a parterre, displaying its
patter under the wide open sky.

Harold Nicholson, gardener and politician
in the introduction to *Great Gardens* by Peter Coats

YOU CAN CALL ME FLOWER IF YOU LIKE

Flowers given the Royal Horticultural Society's Award of Garden
Merit (AGM) with famous namesakes:

Latin Name	Common Name
Brugmansia x candida	Grand Marnier
Callistemon viminalis	Captain Cook
Camellia japonica	Bob Hope
Camellia x williamsii	Brigadoon
Fuchsia	Winston Churchill/Tom Thumb
Begonia	Cleopatra
Bellis perennis	Rob Roy
Lobelia	Queen Victoria
Lupinus	Pope John Paul
Paeonia	Sarah Bernhardt
Dahlia	Rigoletto
Lathyrus odoratus	Pocahontas/Charlie's Angel/Kiri Te Kanawa

WOODWORKING

It takes many different kinds of wood to make a piano. These include:
maple, which is used to eliminate distortion; spruce, a lightweight
wood with great elasticity and an ability to vibrate; lime which
doesn't raise or warp under the key veneers; and ebony, which is used
for the black keys.

Two centuries before modern gardeners noticed that their daylilies closed at night, taxonomist Linnaeus discovered that the petals of many flower species opened and closed at regular times. He even created a garden so that he could tell the time of day by just looking at it.

Since much depended on where the garden was located and how many hours of sunlight it received, Linnaeus's garden was criticised as not being accurate. Many fellow gardeners also declared the clock garden pointless and ugly – Linneaus had grouped plants together based on the time they told, rather than their aesthetic beauty. But the concept has since gained great popularity, and flowering clocks are planted in cities throughout the world. You can make your own floral clock, using the following plants.

1am	*Closes*: Field sowthistle
2am	*Opens*: Yellow goat's-beard
3am	*Opens*: Bristly ox-tongue
4am	*Opens*: Late-flowering dandelion and wild succory
5am	*Opens*: Naked-stalked poppy and smooth sowthistle
6am	*Opens*: Elegant cat's-ears
7am	*Opens*: Garden lettuce and African marigold; *Closes*: Night-flowering catch-fly
8am	*Opens*: Scarlet pimpernel, mouse-ear hawkweed and proliferous pink; *Closes*: Evening primrose
9am	*Opens*: Field marigold; *Closes*: Purple bindweed
10am	*Opens*: Red sandwort; *Closes*: Yellow goat's-beard
11am	*Opens and closes*: Star-of-Bethlehem ('the lady of 11 o'clock')
Noon	*Opens*: Ice plant; *Closes*: Field sowthistle
1pm	*Opens*: Common purslane; *Closes*: Proliferous pink
2pm	*Closes*: Purple sandwort
3pm	*Closes*: Field marigold
4pm	*Closes*: White spadewort and field bindwort
5pm	*Closes*: Elegant cat's-ears
6pm	*Opens*: Dark crane's-bill; *Closes*: White water-lily
7pm	*Closes*: Naked-stalked poppy
8pm	*Closes*: Orange daylily and wild succory
9pm	*Opens*: Prickly pear cactus; *Closes*: *Convolvulus Linnae'us* and chickweed
10pm	*Opens*: Purple bindweed; *Closes*: Common nipplewort
11pm	*Opens*: Night-flowering catch-fly; *Closes*: Smooth sowthistle
Midnight	*Closes*: Creeping mallow and late-flowering dandelion

*There's one good thing about snow, it makes your lawn look as
nice as your neighbour's.*
CLYDE MOORE, gardener

IS IT A CACTUS, OR...

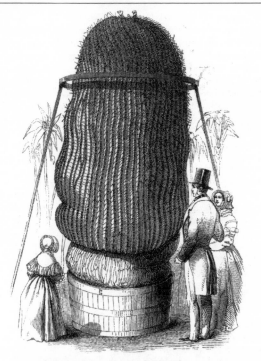

"MONSTER CACTUS," AT THE ROYAL BOTANIC GARDENS, KEW.

*Henry couldn't help smirking as the occupants of the basket
became enveloped by the deflating hot air balloon.*

GARDEN GAGS

What do you call a stolen yam?
A hot potato

SEX AND PLANTS AND ROCK AND ROLL

Guaiacum officinale also known as *Lignum vitae* (wood of life) is a short evergreen that grows in South America. When it was discovered in the 16th century, its resin was thought to be a cure for venereal disease. So popular was it amongst Europeans, it almost became extinct through over-harvesting.

BEDDING DOWN

In **flat beds**, the soil is level with the surrounding garden and should be separated from other beds or lawns with bricks or edging. They hold moisture well and are slow to dry out in spring months.

Raised beds are higher than the surrounding garden and suitable for areas with difficult soils, which the addition of organic material helps to improve. Not only more comfortable to weed, the depth of the soil allows roots to absorb nutrients better. They dry out quicker in spring when the warmth of the soil also gives plants with short growing seasons a head start.

Sunken beds are ideal in warm, dry climates with sandy soils – Native Americans have been using them for hundreds of years. They have lower temperatures than the surrounding garden and are good at soaking in surplus water.

Terraced beds allow cultivation on steeply-sloping land where soil would otherwise erode downhill. Popular amongst dry rice growers in hilly areas, they vastly increase hillside yield.

GARDENERS IN FICTION

Whether attracted by the ideal of self-sufficiency, the snobbery of Margo or the sex appeal of Barbara Good, who hasn't watched *The Good Life*? Even the Queen has admitted to being one of the show's most dedicated fans, tuning in weekly as Tom and Barbara tried to turn their typically middle-class Surbiton home into an urban farm.

QUOTE UNQUOTE

Our England is a garden, and such gardens are not made
By singing 'Oh how beautiful' and sitting in the shade.
RUDYARD KIPLING, writer

ARE YOUR PLANTS HARD ENOUGH?

Plant hardiness tables are designed to ensure gardeners choose the correct plants for the temperature ranges they live in. The most important factor is the minimum range temperature. Global hardiness zones range from minimum temperatures of below -50°F to 40°F and above. Britain is mainly in Zone 6.

Zone	Minimum Temperature
1	Below -50°F
2a	-45°F -to -50°F
2b	-40°F to -45°F
3a	-35°F to -40°F
3b	-30°F to -35°F
4a	-25°F to -30°F
4b	-20°F to -25°F
5a	-15°F to -20°F
5b	-10°F to -15°F
6a	-5°F to -10°F
6b	0°F to -5°F
7a	5°F to 0°F
7b	10°F to 5°F
8a	15°F to 10°F
8b	20°F to 15°F
9a	25°F to 20°F
9b	30°F to 25°F
10a	35°F to 30°F
10b	40°F to 35°F
11	40°F and above

FLYCATCHER!

It is thought that a select group of plants evolved into insectivores because their roots could not absorb sufficient nutrients. Although they can be grown indoors, they are tricky to feed if there are no flies about (they may digest small pieces of meat if really hungry). There are three types:

• Fly traps, such as the Venus fly trap (*Dionaea muscipula*) whose hinged leaves are edged with spines that close instantly when touched by an insect.

• Sticky-leaved plants, such as the rounded-leaved sundew (*Drosera rotundifolia*) whose leaves are covered with hairs that secret insect-catching fluid which traps and digests.

• Pitcher plants such as the cobra pitcher (*Darlingtonia californica*) with water filled-funnels and a poison well which drowns insects.

ORIGIN OF THE SPECIES

Fruit	From	Local Name
Breadfruit	Hawaii	*ulu*
Custard apple	South America	*cherimoya*
Cloudberry	Sweden	*hjortron*
Lingonberry	North America	*cowberry*
Lychee	Southern China	*wai chee*
Japanese medlar	Southern China	*loquat*
Tamarind	Africa	*sampalok*

ON THE GRAPEVINE

One Sunday, in the days of my youth, I was 'volunteered' with my younger brother to superintend the family garden which was opening for a Red Cross Sunday. We had been weeding all morning, and at lunch time handed over to the various dignitaries who set up card tables, arrows to the lavatory, the tea tent and so on. Meanwhile my brother and I lurked in the rhododendrons, ready to tackle cutting pinchers, retrieve lost children, banish unwelcome dogs and generally see to the needs of the public. One of the first to arrive was a famous local Brigadier (retd.) who had a short fuse and tended to speak in telegrams. He obviously disliked teenagers intensely, for he glared at my brother and shouted 'Hostas!'

'Sorry?' queried my brother, who didn't know a dahlia from a damson.

'Where are your hostas?' The Brigadier's face was turning crimson. Clearly, with words at a premium he disliked having to repeat himself.

'They're not here, sir,' said my brother.

'Can see that! That's why I'm asking.'

'They've gone to India. They'll be back next week.'

'Good god!' said the Brigadier and strode off looking perplexed. I looked at my brother.

'What on earth did you say that for?' I asked.

'I thought "hosta" must be a military word for "parent".' He shuffled more deeply into the rhododendrons to hid his embarrassment. Inevitably, the military gent found the hostas and strode back to berate us.

'India be dammed!' he roared. 'Down by pond! Hostas! Dozens! Pretty sight. Lovely kalmias too! Very pretty. That boy your gardener? Useless! No clue!

Nigel Colborn, *Hortus*

ON THE GRAPEVINE

The Minister's answer was to let out a burp, which I considered a very well-spoken reply because it was apparent he was about to throw up. Nobu and I rushed over to help him, but he'd already clamped his hand over his mouth. If he'd been a volcano, he would have been smoking by this time, so we had no choice but to roll open the glass doors to the garden to let him vomit onto the snow there. You may be appalled at the thought of a man throwing up into one of these exquisite decorative gardens, but the Minister certainly wasn't the first. We geisha try to help a man down the hallway to the toilet, but sometimes we can't manage it. If we say to one of the maids that a man has just visited the garden, they all know exactly what we mean and come at once with their cleaning supplies.

Arthur Golden, *Memoirs of a Geisha*

QUOTE UNQUOTE

The Earth is a large garden, and each of us need only care for our own part of life to be breathed back into the planet, into the soil, into ourselves.
JOHN JEAVONS, soil activist

ORIGIN OF THE SPECIES

As English as an oak tree? Some of our most common plants have rather more exotic roots:

Plant Name	Brought to England from
Rhododendron yunnanense	China, Burma, Tibet
Euphorbia sikkimensis	Sikkim (North-east India)
Kniphofia nelsonii	South Africa
Tradescantia virginiana	United States
Clematis montana	Himalayas
Jasminium nudiflorum	China
Wisteria sinensis	China
Kerria japonica	Japan
Narcissus asturiensis	Spain
Dianthus alpinus	Austrian Alps

WHAT IS THE SOIL-FIST TEST?

Take a handful of soil that is slightly moist and crush it in the palm of your hand. If the soil keeps the impressions of your fingers it's clay, if it crumbles immediately it's sand, but if it holds its shape briefly and then crumbles into small chunks, it's loam.

Rose

Roses became an important emblem during Henry VII's marriage to Elizabeth when a rose bush growing in Wiltshire started flowering with mottled red and white blooms. The Tudors adopted it as their symbol in order to unite the houses of York (traditionally a white rose) and Lancaster (traditionally a red rose). Classified as *Rosa x damascena var versicolor*, the mottled red and white rose is still grown today.

The Thistle

Scotland is believed to have taken the thistle as their official flower after a 1263 battle between Scottish and Danish soldiers. Legend has it that the Danes attempted to mount a surprise attack under cover of darkness, only to be thwarted in the attempt when one of their men stepped on a thistle and howled loudly with pain.

Broom

The Plantagenet family adopted broom (*Planta genista*) as their badge of honour after Geoffrey of Anjou picked a sprig on his way to battle in the 12th century.

The Leek

The Welsh are said to have adopted the leek as their national symbol during an ancient battle with the Saxons. Both sides were clad in chain-mail and helmets, which made it impossible to tell who was friend or enemy. Quicker on the uptake, the Welsh soldiers pulled some leeks from a nearby cottage garden and stuck them in their helmets, enabling them to concentrate on killing the Saxons, while the Saxons continued to attack their own side.

Fleur-de-lys

This familiar design is a stylised representation of the 'fleur de luce', the common wild iris that grows in swamps. According to legend, the 6th century French King Clovis faced death when his retreat from battle was cut off by a river. By tracing his way through wild iris, his army followed a shallow route to safety, and in gratitude, he adopted the flower as his emblem.

LONDON'S SECRET GARDENS

Found 100ft above street level on the roof of a department store in Kensington, there's a 1.5-acre walled secret that goes by the name of Derry and Tom's Garden. It's inspired by the Moorish architecture and plantings of Southern Spain, with white-washed walls, exotic palms, trickling fountains and colourful glazed tiles.

Cost, in thousands of pounds, of building the 'great stove' at Chatsworth

WHERE HAVE ALL THE APPLES GONE?

The wild apple, known by its Latin name *Malus sieversii*, is the daddy of apples. It originated in Kazakhstan and was an early traveller, making its way along the Silk Road to Europe. It arrived in Rome at the height of the Roman Empire and appeared in Britain shortly after. The oldest variety grown in Britain is the pearmain, also known as the great pear apple, which has been traced back to 1200 AD.

Queen Charlotte, wife of George III is credited with introducing the Queen's apple, also known as Borsdörfer or Edelborsdörfer, from northern Germany to Britain, where it was first grown at Brompton Park Nursery in 1785. Charlotte, known to be partial to a good firm German apple had hundreds brought over from Germany and cooked into a pudding that became known as the Apple Charlotte.

Over 6,000 varieties of apple have been grown in England, yet in our supermarkets today the British apple fights for shelf space among foreign varieties that have been flown thousands of miles. Next time you decide to eat an apple, make it one of the home-grown varieties.

BLOOMING PUZZLES

I am black of eye and bright of hair.
I stick into the ground yet I follow my bright lord
as he races around the sky.
What am I?
Answer on page 153

POISONOUS PLANTS

In *Moonraker*, James Bond (Roger Moore) discovers a toxic nerve gas in the laboratories of Hugo Drax, which is deadly poisonous to humans, but not to animals. When analysed, the gas is found to have come from from *Orchidae negra*, a black orchid that was found in the area of the River Tapirape in South America. What does Hugo Drax, the psychotic billionaire obsessed with space want with *Orchidae negra*? Well to destroy the human population of course.

In real life, however, things are somewhat less dramatic. There are indeed several varieties of black orchid, but not one of them is called *Orchidae negra*.

TOP OF THE GRASS

The Royal Horticultural Society's Award of Garden Merit recognises 'plants of excellence' in gardens. It provides a practical guide to gardeners faced with a bewildering variety of plants to choose from. Awards are either made after a trial at Wisley or by recommendation from a panel of experts. Any type of plant, fruit or vegetable qualifies, from a tiny delicate alpine to a giant tree, as long as it satisfies the following criteria:

The plant should:
• Be suitable for ordinary garden use (either in the open, or under glass)
• Be of good constitution
• Be available in the horticultural trade or available for propagation

The plant should not:
• Be susceptible to any pest or disease
• Require highly specialised care other than the provision of appropriate growing conditions (eg lime-free soil when required)
• Be subject to an unreasonable degree of reversion in its vegetative or floral categories

QUOTE UNQUOTE

Gardening requires lots of water – most of it in the form of perspiration.
LOU ERICKSON, critic and poet

LOVE DANGEROUSLY

For a male garden spider, courting is a very dangerous business that requires tact, delicacy and quick thinking. Since a male spider is smaller than a female, who has a somewhat violent reputation, he can risk death if he enters her web unannounced.

Proceeding cautiously is the only option. Ever fearful, most male spiders play it safe by approaching the female's web with a getaway clause – a thread with which to drop down quickly if his suit proves unwelcome. If he survives the initial approach, next comes the tricky part. First he must subdue and entice her onto a special breeding thread, then he has to attempt the hazardous job of inserting one of his palps, already charged with semen, into her body and then, if he's lucky, he must insert the other before making a quick getaway.

A male garden spider has to be particularly careful in autumn when weakened by lack of food, he will most likely end up as a post-coital picnic. But all is not lost, for his body, when ingested, will help nourish his offspring.

ON THE GRAPEVINE

Beyond his hope, Eve separate he spies,
Veiled in a cloud of fragrance, where she stood,
Half spied, so thick the roses blushing round
About her glowed, oft stooping to support
Each flower of slender stalk, whose head, though gay
Carnation, purple, azure, or specked with gold,
Hung drooping unsustained; them she upstays
Gently with myrtle band, mindless the while
Herself, though fairest unsupported flower,
From her best prop so far, and storm so nigh.
Nearer he drew, and many a walk traversed
Of stateliest covert, cedar, pine, or palm;
Then voluble and bold, now hid, now seen,
Among thick-woven arborets, and flowers
Imbordered on each bank

John Milton, *Paradise Lost, Book IX*

FLOWERS OF THE ZODIAC

Capricorn	Dec 21 – Jan 19	Chrysanthemum
Aquarius	Jan 20 – Feb 18	Daffodil
Pisces	Feb 19 – Mar 20	Freesia
Aries	Mar 21 – Apr 20	Tulip
Taurus	Apr 21 – May 20	Iris
Gemini	May 21 – Jun 20	Alstroemeria
Cancer	Jun 21 – Jul 21	Rose
Leo	Jul 22 – Aug 21	Carnation
Virgo	Aug 22 – Sept 22	Gladiolus
Libra	Sept 23 – Oct 22	Dahlia
Scorpio	Oct 23 – Nov 21	Gerbera daisy
Sagittarius	Nov 22 – Dec 20	Anemone

SEEDY TERMINOLOGY

Adpressed – a part of a plant pressed close to another organ, usually hairs pressed close to stems or leaves

Drupe – a plant with fleshy fruit that encloses one or more seeds, for example a cherry

Panicle – a plant with many small branchlets of flowers

Mericarp – a one-seeded portion of fruit which splits off from the plant

Peduncle – a flower that divides into many different stems and flowerets

Whorl – a plant with two organs (usually leaves) that grow at the same point on its stem

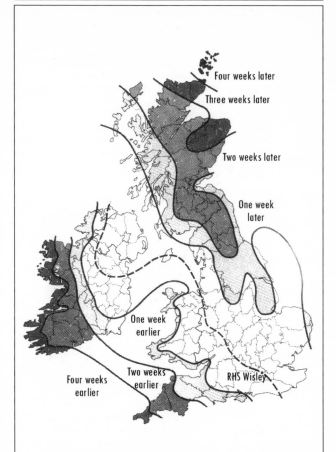

*Spring arrives first in Cornwall and proceeds through the
south-west corner of England and South Wales, reaching RHS
Wisley – the centre of the gardening calendar – before gradually
progressing north. In the Orkneys, spring finally
arrives a full eight weeks after Cornwall. On higher ground,
there is also a time-lag; it is generally about two days for every
hundred feet rise in height.*

COME into the garden, Maud,
  For the black bat, night, has flown,
Come into the garden, Maud,
  I am here at the gate alone;
And the woodbine spices are wafted abroad,
  And the musk of the rose is blown.

For a breeze of morning moves,
  And the planet of Love is on high,
Beginning to faint in the light that she loves
  On a bed of daffodil sky,
To faint in the light of the sun she loves,
  To faint in his light, and to die.

All night have the roses heard
  The flute, violin, bassoon;
All night has the casement jessamine stirr'd
  To the dancers dancing in tune;
Till silence fell with the waking bird,
  And a hush with the setting moon.

I said to the lily, 'There is but one
  With whom she has heart to be gay.
When will the dancers leave her alone?
  She is weary of dance and play.'
Now half to the setting moon are gone,
  And half to the rising day;
Low on the sand and loud on the stone
  The last wheel echoes away.

I said to the rose, 'The brief night goes
  In babble and revel and wine.
O young lord-lover, what sighs are those,
  For one that will never be thine
But mine, but mine,' I sware to the rose,
  'For ever and ever, mine.'

And the soul of the rose went into my blood,
  As the music clash'd in the hall:
And long by the garden lake I stood,
  For I heard your rivulet fall
From the lake to the meadow and on to the wood,
  Our wood, that is dearer than all;

From the meadow your walks have left so sweet
  That whenever a March-wind sighs
He sets the jewel-print of your feet
  In violets blue as your eyes,
To the woody hollows in which we meet
  And the valleys of Paradise.

The slender acacia would not shake
  One long milk-bloom on the tree;
The white lake-blossom fell into the lake
  As the pimpernel doz'd on the lea;
But the rose was awake all night for your sake,
  Knowing your promise to me;
The lilies and roses were all awake,
  They sigh'd for the dawn and thee.

Queen rose of the rosebud garden of girls,
  Come hither, the dances are done,
In gloss of satin and glimmer of pearls,
  Queen lily and rose in one;
Shine out, little head, sunning over with curls,
  To the flowers, and be their sun.

There has fallen a splendid tear
  From the passion-flower at the gate.
She is coming, my dove, my dear;
  She is coming, my life, my fate;
The red rose cries, 'She is near, she is near;'
  And the white rose weeps, 'She is late;'
The larkspur listens, 'I hear, I hear;'
  And the lily whispers, 'I wait.'

She is coming, my own, my sweet;
  Were it ever so airy a tread,
My heart would hear her and beat,
  Were it earth in an earthy bed;
My dust would hear her and beat,
  Had I lain for a century dead;
Would start and tremble under her feet,
  And blossom in purple and red.

Alfred Lord Tennyson, *Maud*

Maud won't come into the garden
Maud is compelled to state.
Though you stand for hours in among the flowers
Down by the garden gate.
Maud won't come into the garden,
Sing to her as you may.
Maud says she begs your pardon
But she wasn't born yesterday.

But Maud's not coming into the garden
Thanking you just the same.
Though she looks so pure, you may be quite sure
Maud's on to your little game.
Maud knows she's being dampening,
And how damp you already must be,
So Maudie is now decamping
To her lovely hot water b.

Frankly Maud wouldn't dream of coming into the garden,
Let that be understood,
When the nights are warm, Maud knows the form,
Maud has read 'Little Red Riding Hood'.
Maud did not need much warning,
She watched you with those pink gins
So she bids you a kind 'Good Morning'
And advises you two aspirins.

You couldn't really seriously think that Maud was going
    to be such a sucker as to come into the garden,
Flowers set her teeth on edge
And she's much too old for the strangle hold
In a prickly privet hedge.
Pray stand till your arteries harden
It won't do the slightest good,
Maud is not coming into the garden
And you're mad to have thought she would

Joyce Grenfell, *Maud Replies*

QUOTE UNQUOTE

I'm not really a career person. I'm a gardener, basically.
GEORGE HARRISON, the quiet Beatle

40 *Maximum number of daily sit-ups new gardeners should do for one to two weeks before going out into the garden according to Dr Peter Skew*

THERE'S ALWAYS A WORT FOR IT

There are more than 400 examples of plants ending in the suffix wort. Wort comes from old English meaning root:

Bladderwort..................an insecticide plant, with bladder-shaped leaves that animals become trapped in
Barrenwort ....a plant thought to be the cause of infertility
Birthwort...............................a plant used in childbirth to ease delivery
Butterwort........a bog plant with a reputation for keeping cows in milk
Nipplewort..................................a plant reputed to treat breast tumours
Figwort ....a plant originally used for treating piles (which were referred to as figs for their similarity in shape)
Fleawort..............a plant with a dubious reputation for destroying fleas
Lungwort....................a plant with leaves that resemble a diseased lung
Motherwort...........................a plant used to treat diseases of the uterus
Mugwort...........................a plant with a reputation for repelling midges
Ragwort......................................a plant whose leaves have ragged edges
Rupturewort ....a plant with a reputation for curing hernias
Sneezewort ....a plant whose dried leaves are used to prevent sneezing
Stitchwort..........a plant with a reputation for curing stitches in the side
St John's wort ....the best known of the worts, which is reputed to flower on the feast day of St John the Baptist (24th June)
Spiderwort ....a plant believed to be named after its spidery shape
Swallowwort..............................a plant that blossoms with the return of swallows in spring

QUOTE UNQUOTE

Of all the wonders of nature, a tree in summer is perhaps the most remarkable; with the possible exception of a moose singing 'Embraceable You' in spats.
WOODY ALLEN, director

THE FLOWERING OF AGES

530 million years ago, there were very few plants; generally only seaweeds and non-flowering plants that lived in water. About 200 million years later, the earliest plants landed. They were ferns with stiff stems and anchoring roots, cycads and cone-bearers.

Development was slow, and it wasn't until the Jurassic Period (from 195 to 136 million years ago) that the first plants flowered – an abrupt and surprising development that provided seeds with a far greater chance of survival. But how did flowers grow? The details are imprecise but it is thought that petals grew up from modified leaves and nectar came about from production of excess sugar.

PLANT PANACEA

Four plants that have lengthened lives

Sphagnum moss is able to absorb up to 20 times its own weight in water and contains antibiotic fungi. Used as far back as the Bronze Age to heal wounds, it is still used by injured soldiers to staunch bleeding on the battlefield.

In the 1950s, the **rosy periwinkle** (*Catharanthus roseus*), a member of the poisonous dogbane family, was discovered to have two alkaloids, vincristine and vinblastine, which are effective against certain types of cancer cells and are used in the treatment of leukaemia, sarcoma, Hodgkin's disease, and cancers of the breast and testicle.

The **common yew** (*Taxus baccata*) is also important in the fight against cancer. The critical compound is paclitaxel, which was originally found in tiny amounts in the bark of the pacific yew. But one 60-year-old tree can only yield enough paclitaxel to treat a single patient and large-scale logging in the 1980s threatened the supply of the drug. Fortunately a precursor to paclitaxel was discovered in the leaves of the common yew.

The **common British foxglove** (*Digitalis purpurea*) has saved millions of heart disease sufferers by strengthening the heart's muscular activity and regulating dangerously fast heartbeats. The Austrian foxglove (*Digitalis ianata*) contains a greater concentration of digitalis from the glycosides on its leaves and as neither can be synthesised, both types are grown commercially.

BLOOMING PUZZLES

I thrive in winter,
die in summer
and grow with my roots upwards.
What am I?
Answer on page 153

KEY TO THE MAZE

The world's largest water maze is in the Parc de la Mer, St Helier, Jersey. It consists of 208 fountain jets that ebb and flow to create walls of water that form cells within the maze and 'doorways', which appear and disappear from moment to moment. The maze measures 20m across, and its fountain configuration alters every 30 minutes. It's best to visit on a warm day with a towel!

The Wardian Case was invented in 1827 when a London physician called Nathaniel Ward placed a caterpillar and a piece of mould in a glass jar as an experiment.

According to the legend, he forgot about it, only to come across it sometime later to discover a small fern and a blade of grass growing out of the mould. There is no record of what happened to the caterpillar.

His discovery led to the invention of the Wardian Case, which is now used to transport exotic plants over long distances. This so revolutionised the world of plant hunting that some refer to plant hunting before 1834, as pre-Wardian, and collecting after 1834, as post-Wardian, so ushering in an era when plants were collected and dispersed all over the world.

What should you do if you find some edible looking mushrooms in your compost heap? Don't cook or eat them! In Oregon, USA in 1988, a housewife cooked up a plate of death caps, mistakenly believing they were harmless paddy straw mushrooms. The result? Four out of the five diners were rushed to hospital for liver transplants. To ensure an altogether more pleasant ending to a meal with hand-picked mushrooms, remember this salutary fact: 20 to 30% of pickers who mistakenly consume death caps will be eating their last meal.

There is no rule of thumb for identifying whether a mushroom is poisonous or not, and each offering needs to be accurately identified. Old wives' tales should be taken with a pinch of salt: just because your pet can eat it and survive, doesn't mean you will. Rabbits, for example have different digestive systems and are able to eat many types of poisonous mushrooms without side-effects. And don't put your faith in poisonous mushrooms turning blue when cooked (as another saying goes) – and they won't turn garlic or parsley black, tarnish silver spoons or curdle milk either.

Amongst the inedible fungi listed below are a few deadly poisonous ones and one intriguing specimen which cannot be eaten with alcohol.

Mushroom	Side-effects
Death cap	Death through liver or kidney failure. This variety is the cause of most fatalities, generally knocking off one third of those foolish enough to eat it and it doesn't end there – even putting one in your basket can spread its poisonous spores onto anything around it. If you ever pick one, discard it immediately and wash your hands thoroughly.
Fly agaric	This red and white spotted variety goes straight for the central nervous system causing euphoria, hallucinations, intoxication, hyperactivity, coma and possibly death.
Yellow stainer	The cold sweats and stomach pains start soon after eating, and quick treatment is needed to avoid serious respiratory difficulties and digestive problems. Oddly, some people are unaffected.
Destroying angel	Be very wary, this white fungus can be easily confused for some varieties of edible mushroom. Once eaten its toxins are similar to the death cap and just as deadly.

44 *Weight, in pounds, of the giant fan palm seed, which can take 10 years to develop and is the largest in the world*

White coral	Although it's not poisonous, you wouldn't want to taste the bitter flavour of this mushroom.
Satan's bolete	Severe stomach upsets, nausea, cramps and vomiting have all been recorded although some do insist that this member of the *Boletus* family is edible after hours of cooking.
Common ink cap	Hot flushes, nausea and palpitations are just some of the effects caused when taken with alcohol. It's also wise to avoid alcohol during subsequent meals. A chemical substance with similar properties is used for treating alcoholics.
False morel	Raw, these mushrooms are very poisonous. They are still eaten by some after thoroughly boiling or drying but it's probably best not to risk it.
False chanterelle	Originally declared poisonous, then safe, these mushrooms should only be eaten in small quantities to avoid digestive complaints. They're easy to confuse with the true chanterelle.
Sulphur tuft	Very bitter to eat, this mushroom's side-effects are serious with severe stomach effects that can be sometimes fatal.
Woolly milk cap	Bitter, acrid and peppery to taste, diarrhoea and vomiting are just some of the recorded side-effects.
Jack o'lantern	These bright orange mushrooms have gills that glow in the dark. When eaten they can cause stomach cramps, vomiting and diarrhoea. Fortunately, they are rare in Britain.
Common earthball	Although not deadly, the earthball does cause serious problems to the digestive system.
Bitter bolete	Although not actually poisonous, this bolete is so bitter that the presence of a single mushroom will make a whole dish inedible.

GARDENING BY THE BOOK

Britain's best known gardening society, the Royal Horticultural Society (RHS) was formed on 7 March 1804 at the home of James Hatchards, the bookshop owner, at 187 Piccadilly, London.

ON THE GRAPEVINE

Already it was deep summer on roadhouse roofs and in front of way-side garages, where new red petrol-pumps sat out in pools of light and when I reached my estate at West Egg I ran the car under its shed and sat for a while on an abandoned grass roller in the yard. The wind had blown off, leaving a loud bright night, with wings beating in the trees and a persistent organ sound as the full bellows of the earth blew the frogs full of life. The silhouette of a moving cat wavered across the moonlight, and, turning my head to watch it, I saw that I was not alone – fifty feet away a figure had emerged from the shadow of my neighbour's mansion and was standing with his hands in his pockets regarding the silver pepper of the stars. Something in his leisurely movements and the secure position of his feet upon the lawn suggested that it was Mr Gatsby himself, come out to determine what share was his of our local heavens.

I decided to call him. Miss Baker had mentioned him at dinner, and that would do for an introduction. But I didn't call to him, for he gave a sudden intimation that he was content to be alone – he stretched out his arms toward the dark water in a curious way, and, far as I was from him, I could have sworn he was trembling. Involuntarily I glanced seaward – and distinguished nothing except a single green light, minute and far away, that might have been the end of a dock. When I looked once more for Gatsby he had vanished and I was alone again in the unquiet darkness.

F Scott Fitzgerald, *The Great Gatsby*

TEN ORNAMENTAL GRASSES

Corkscrew rush	*Juncus effusus 'Spiralis'*
Japanese blood grass	*Imperata cylindrica 'Red baron'*
Purple moor grass	*Molinia caerulea*
Switch grass	*Panicum virgatum*
Fountain grass	*Pennisetum setaceum*
Ribbon grass	*Phalaris arundinacea*
Tufted hairgrass	*Deschampsia cespitosa*
Blue oat grass	*Helictotrichon sempervirens*
Maiden grass	*Miscanthus sinensis*
Dwarf bamboo	*Sasaella hidaensis muraii*

QUOTE UNQUOTE

Flowers are restful to look at. They have neither emotions nor conflicts.
SIGMUND FREUD, psychologist

46 *Number of different butterfly species recorded in British gardens in 2001 by Butterfly Conservation*

WHY DO LEAVES CHANGE COLOUR?

During spring and summer, leaves absorb energy from the sun to turn carbon dioxide and water into carbohydrates (sugar and starch). The chemical responsible for this transformation is chlorophyll, and it is also this chemical which turns them green. The green pigment is so strong it also masks other coloured pigments, such as the orange carotene, which is present but unseen. In autumn, the reduction in sunlight hours and temperature causes leaves to stop absorbing the sun's energy, and the chlorophyll breaks down, making way for the other pigments to change the leaf colour. The degree of red is also affected by temperature, light and water supply. Low autumn temperatures above freezing encourage reds to deepen, but temperatures below freezing reduce reds, and on overcast and rainy days, the colour in the leaves is intensified.

THE LANDSCAPE ARCHITECTS' LANDSCAPE ARCHITECT

Joseph Paxton, one of Britain's favourite garden designers, is believed to have been born in 1801 (he might have fibbed a little to get his first job). Despite being born into poverty and untrained, Paxton died in 1865, having laid out the extraordinary gardens at Chatsworth, designed and built the Crystal Palace, started up the long-running *Gardener's Chronicle*, founded the *Daily News* newspaper, served as an MP and built up a fortune equivalent to £8.5 million today.

Among Paxton's achievements at Chatsworth are the enormous fountains (one is twice the height of Nelson's Column), the arboretum and the 300ft glass conservatory, known at the time as the 'great stove'. But it was his inspired design for a crystal palace for the 1851 Great Exhibition that brought lasting fame. Following the rejection of all the 245 designs submitted, and public disapproval of the committee's own offering, Paxton took nine days to design a vast glass house, based on the lily house at Chatsworth, which was cheap, easy to construct and easy to remove. It may have been publicly derided when it was first erected, but unlike the Millennium Dome, it quickly became a winner.

Sadly, the great stove at Chatsworth proved too expensive to heat and was destroyed in 1923. You can't visit the Crystal Palace either, it was burnt down in an accident in 1936. However, Paxton's influences in the fields of gardening, architecture and engineering remain to this day.

CELEBRITY GARDENERS

Once best known as the singer of *Kids in America* (who could forget that thick black eyeliner and once-fashionable mullet?), **Kim Wilde** has since cut her hair, hung up her microphone and relaunched herself into an entirely different creative pursuit. What started off as a passion for gardening has earned her a place as the resident designer on *Garden Invaders* and a regular column in *The Guardian*. She also designed a show garden at the RHS Tatton Hall Flower Show which, based around *Alice Through the Looking Glass*, was voted the best garden of the show.

REASONS TO KEEP OUT OF THE GARDEN

Alliumphobia ....a fear of garlic
Amathophobia ....a fear of dust
Anthrophobia ....a fear of flowers
Arachnophobia ....a fear of spiders
Astraphobia ....a fear of thunder and lightning
Automysophobia ....a fear of being dirty
Botanophobia ....a fear of plants
Bufonophobia ....a fear of toads
Dendrophobia ....a fear of trees
Doraphobia ....a fear of fur or skins of animals
Entomophobia ....a fear of insects
Eosophobia ....a fear of dawn or daylight
Felinophobia ....a fear of cats
Frigophobia ....a fear of the cold
Heliophobia ....a fear of the sun

ON THE GRAPEVINE

Timmy Willie longed to be at home in his peaceful nest in a sunny bank. The food disagreed with him; the noise prevented him from sleeping. In a few days he grew so thin that Johnny Town-mouse noticed it, and questioned him. He listened to Timmy Willie's story and inquired about the garden. 'It sounds rather a dull place? What do you do when it rains?'

'When it rains, I sit in my little sandy burrow and shell corn and seeds from my Autumn store. I peep out at the throstles and blackbirds on the lawn, and my friend Cock Robin. And when the sun comes out again, you should see my garden and the flowers – roses and pinks and pansies – no noise except the birds and bees, and the lambs in the meadows.'

Beatrix Potter, *The Tale of Johnny Town-Mouse*

RABBITING ON

Richard Adams' 1972 best-selling novel *Watership Down* followed a group of rabbits (who are named after plants), as they leave their warren on the advice of a prophetic rabbit named Fiver (who isn't). On their journey to find a new home, they encounter difficulties and adventures, before eventually establishing a new warren on Watership Down, a hill which actually exists on the outskirts of Newbury.

Some of the *Dramatis rabbitae*:

Hazel	The quietly confident leader of the group who sets out to form a new warren
Fiver	Hazel's brother, with a gift for seeing into the future
Bigwig	The big rabbit, named after a tuft of fur on his head
Blackberry	Good at getting the others out of scrapes and named after the black tips on the ends of his ears
Dandelion	A fast runner who entertains the rest of the rabbits with his stories of rabbit heaven
Silver	A prematurely grey rabbit who falls in with the group to get away from bullying
Holly	A fighter rabbit who initially resists joining the group, but finds them later
Cowslip	An outsider, who joins the group and uses his big size and eloquence to gain acceptance
Strawberry	Another outsider with a talent for digging warrens and a keenness for bunny architecture
General Woundwort	A huge and violent rabbit who very nearly frustrates the rabbits' search for mates
Blackavar	A subdued rabbit whose ears were shredded during a fight in his own warren
Kehaar	An injured gull nursed to health by the rabbits. He repays the favour by helping them in their search for females. Named for his call, not a plant.

ON THE GRAPEVINE

Oberon: I pray thee, give it me. I know a bank where the wild thyme blows, Where oxlips and the nodding violet grows, Quite over-canopied with luscious woodbine, With sweet musk-roses and with eglantine: There sleeps Titania sometime of the night, Lull'd in these flowers with dances and delight...

William Shakespeare,
A Midsummer Night's Dream, Act II, Scene 1

*Number of order beds which contain plants grown according to their 49
botanical classification in the Chelsea Physic Garden*

SLOW DEVELOPER

The rare Bolivian herb, *Puya raimondii* was first discovered in 1870. Never one in a hurry, *Puya raimondii* grows steadily for 150 years, develops a panicle and then dies off. How scientists know it takes 150 years to flower is a bit of a mystery; it is only 134 years since the plant was discovered.

GNOMES GNOTES

The 90s feel-good British flick, *The Full Monty*, featured a much-maligned miniature crew of garden gnomes who sat perkily in the front garden of Gerald, the aspiring former factory foreman. A gnome fanatic, Gerald had acquired a substantial collection of fishermen, chimney-sweeps and miners, from which his fellow strippers derived great amusement. But the little fellow's reputation for industriousness brought little luck for Gerald! During one job interview, two of his gnomes appeared (courtesy of his 'friends') at the window in an off-the-cuff Punch and Judy show. In his confusion at seeing his gnomes at play, Gerald broke into a cold sweat and lost the job: unfortunate for Gerald's wife, but good news for the nation's favourite strippers, as Gerald was the ballroom dancer who dreamt up those bare-all routines.

CAT MINT

If you set it the cats will eat it
If you sow it, the cats don't know it.

Catnip (*Nepeta cataria*) is a wild English plant closely related to mint. It has a peppery scent, particularly fascinating to cats who will destroy and eat any part of it that has been bruised.

And strangely enough this saying seems to be true; cats will destroy any plant that has been bruised or withered – which often happens to plants in the garden – yet cats will ignore any undamaged plants. It seems that nepetalactone, the plant's main chemical (and also a very effective insect repellent), induces in moggies a compulsive-addictive behaviour. So a newly-planted catnip will be unlikely to survive the night if there are cats in the vicinity. As soon as cats in the neighbourhood smell the catnip they will become mesmerised, try to eat it, roll in it, and go all dreamy.

This makes it a very useful plant for catching cats, or even persuading your straying moggie to return to the house. If you have a cat, grow the plant indoors out of reach, and give it some bruised leaves every so often for a treat.

THE OPERA GARDENS AT GLYNDEBOURNE

The famous opera gardens at Glyndebourne in Sussex are thought to have first been laid out in Elizabethan times. However like many gardens, they have been remodelled many times over the years. The current gardens were transformed in the 1930s when John Christie, Glyndebourne's owner, decided to build an opera house in 1932. The gardens were laid out by a talented head gardener known as Mr Harvey. Mr Harvey was famous for his taciturn defence of the gardens – not only did he prevent the architect from building a summer-house that would have closed off the view across the downs, but, according to the Christie family he refused to speak to the stage's carpenter at all. His vigorous protection has not passed unappreciated – for anyone coming to an opera at Glyndebourne's summer season, an elaborate picnic in the beautiful gardens is *de rigueur*.

The gardens contain some very fine old trees, including mulberry, lime, beech, elm and chestnut. The gardens are a beautiful example of unplanned landscape and consequently offer a wide range of garden styles. These include enclosures and open lawns, small formal walled gardens echoing a Tudor style, 18th century picturesque landscapes, lavish herbaceous borders, flowery terraces and vistas reminiscent of the 17th century. Music plays a central role in the gardens – from the sight of the orchestra with their instruments hurrying to the theatre, to distant notes from the practice rooms, or sweet arias reverberating in opera lovers' minds while picnicking during the supper interval.

There is also a variety of different types of wildlife in the gardens including mallards, herons, Canada geese, owls, yellowhammers and wagtails as well as rarer nightingales and moorhens who have relocated from Bentley Wildfowl Park nearby.

Butterflies include tortoiseshells and orange-tips and on some evenings moths include privet and convolvulus hawkmoths. In addition, there are the bats – notorious for getting into the opera house and sometimes swooping down onto the stage during performances.

PLANTS TO MAKE A BEELINE FOR

If you want to attract bees to your garden, plant white, purple, blue and yellow flowers. Bees are very good at seeing ultraviolet colours, and will go straight for them. Plants to attract bees include:

bluebells • bugle • rosemary
dead-nettle • geraniums • foxglove
honeysuckle • monkshood

QUOTE UNQUOTE

I would have liked that man of yours for one of my generals.
THE DUKE OF WELLINGTON, praising Joseph Paxton to the
Duke of Devonshire

ON THE GRAPEVINE

While working in the garden recently, I dug up
a small fragment of truth.

It was adherent all over with clay, and must have been
buried for many years, but I recognised what it was almost at once.

At first we kept it on the mantelpiece in the living room,
but it was often embarrassing to visitors and I eventually
put it on my desk in the study, for a paper-weight.

I asked several close friends what they thought I ought to do
with it, but no one was sure. 'Keep it for your children,'
some said, 'It is a great curiosity.' Others suggested
the local museum.

It was too heavy to take with us when we went on our holidays.
While we were gone, someone broke into the house and stole it.
The police said they would make investigations,
and asked me, 'Could you identify it again as yours, if you
saw it?'

Perhaps. But I'm not sure if I do want it back. After all,
if whoever it was should have found some use for it…
Gael Turnbull, *A Fragment of Truth*

A ROSE-TINTED ORGY

That the Romans were fond of their roses is widely known. But
sometimes their cult of the rose was taken a few stems too far.
Heliogabalus (204-222 AD) was an emperor known mainly for his
debauchery and culinary excesses. However he made it into the history
books because he is held responsible for smothering two of his guests
to death with rose petals during an orgy. The unfortunate pair were
apparently buried under a great weight of the petals that cascaded from
the imperial ceilings.

Non-hybrid (open-pollinated) seeds can be saved, dried and germinated again. Traditionally gardeners have saved seeds for centuries and it's a good way of sharing difficult-to-find varieties and heirlooms with friends that you can't find in nurseries. Saved seeds always seem to grow stronger, flower more and taste better! And if you're an organic gardener, your produce will be free from any chemicals or synthetics.

Harvest your seeds when their pods begin to dry out and crack up. Ensure they don't blow away by covering the seed heads with cheesecloth. Remove pulp from fleshy seeds by soaking them in water in an airtight glass container until they sink. To dry seeds, spread them out in a place where air freely circulates for a week or more. To check whether your seeds are dry enough, put them in an airtight glass jar and place in a warm spot for five minutes. If any condensation appears, they need more drying out.

Store seeds in an envelope (don't forget to label them!) and keep in a cool dark place. Most seeds will last for years if properly dried and stored.

The life of a vegetable seed

One to two years
Onion, parsnip, sweetcorn

Three years
Beans, leek, parsley, pea, pepper

Four years
Beetroot, carrot, pumpkin, tomato

Five years
Broccoli, brussels sprouts, cabbage,
cauliflower, chinese cabbage, lettuce,
melon, radish, turnip

Six years
Celery, cucumber, marrow

QUOTE UNQUOTE

What this country needs is dirtier fingernails
and cleaner minds.
WILL ROGERS, US humorist

WORMS GLORIOUS WORMS

An acre of soil can hold more than a million earthworms.

SPREADING YOUR SEEDS

Bignonia seeds are known as gliders. Gliders have papery wings on either side of the seed which enable them to glide gently down to earth

Silver maple seeds, like the seeds of the European sycamore are known as whirlybirds, one seeded fruits with a single papery wing that rotates like a helicopter blade

Hop tree seeds are known as spinners. The papery membrane surrounding the seed twists and spins through the air.

Dandelion seeds are parachuters with silky tufts on top of the seeds which lift them through the air

BLOOMING PUZZLES

Homophones are words that sound the same but have different meanings. Find two homophones in the following sentence.
Can you cook with something that grows in the garden?
Answer on page 153

54 *Percentage of people who said they had avoided using pesticides in the garden on a regular basis in a recent survey*

BONFIRE ETIQUETTE

Garden bonfires can seriously upset neighbours – particularly someone sitting outside in the sun or hanging up their clean washing, or even an upstairs neighbour with their windows open on a hot day. And if you site your bonfire close to a neighbour's property, the fire could spread. If a bonfire interferes with a neighbour's quiet enjoyment of their property and is frequently lit, the emissions and smoke can be classed as causing a statutory nuisance under the 1990 *Environmental Protection Act*. Neighbours from Hell is an organisation designed to help people avoid falling out with their neighbours. Before lighting a fire they advise you to:

1. Agree a good time and site for the fire with neighbours
2. Keep it away from any boundary fences
3. Make sure it is not situated near any chemicals which could catch fire
4. Keep watching your bonfire to ensure it doesn't get out of control and make sure you have water on hand just in case
5. Don't light it if a neighbour has just put their washing out
6. Don't burn wet garden waste, or materials which cause smoke or fumes
7. Don't situate your fire near a road as smoke could restrict drivers' vision and cause accidents.

ORNAMENTAL CABBAGE

Ornamental cabbage and kale glow brightly in winter beds and containers. Grown as annuals, they come in a variety of colours and leaf shapes. Flowering cabbage has broad, flat, leaves, while kale leaves are curly and frilly around the edges. The plants come in shades of white, green, pink, coral, purple, and red – colours which intensify as temperatures drop below 50°F. To keep the plants thriving, remove their lower leaves as they begin to fade. Plant them in a sunny position in late summer to avoid pests and space them approximately 12 inches apart.

Three of the best to look for are:

Osaka – very fast growing hybrid with bluish green outer leaves and pink or red centres.

Peacock – a very showy hybrid with fine feathery red or white leaves.

Tokyo – perfectly rounded with blue-green outer leaves and soft pink, red, or white centres.

HOSTILE TAKEOVER BID

According to a 2003 study, Britain's rivers and wild lands are being overrun and its native species smothered. The culprits are alien plants such as Japanese knotweed, which have been imported by garden centres and planted by gardeners with a taste for the exotic. The plants have consequently got out into the wild where they are doing their best to take over.

The charity Plantlife says almost all of lowland Britain has been invaded by these unwanted immigrants and their rapacious spread has become one of the greatest obstacles to Britain's natural diversity. When researchers examined the seriousness of the problem, they discovered 82% of the country was suffering under at least one of the invading species. If you are interested in foreign exotics, think carefully before buying imported plants and avoid plants that are invasive. Don't believe you can contain it; just a fingertip of Japanese knotweed is enough for a plant to grow and take over.

The top 12 invasive species are:

Australian swamp stonecrop/
New Zealand pigmyweed ....*Crassula helmsii*
Parrots feather ....*Myriophyllum aquaticum*
Floating pennywort ....*Hydrocotyle ranunculoides*
Japanese knotweed ....*Fallopia japonica*
Waterferns ....*Azolla filiculoides and A. caroliniana*
Indian/Himalayan balsam ....*Impatiens glandulifera*
Water lettuce ....*Pistia stratiotes*
Giant salvinia ....*Salvinia molesta*
Water hyacinth ....*Eichhornia crassipes*
Water chestnut ....*Trapa natans*
Canadian waterweed ....*Elodea canadensis*
Curly waterweed ....*Lagarosiphon major*

ON THE GRAPEVINE

Gardeners are – let's face it – control freaks. Who else would willingly spend his leisure hours wresting weeds out of the ground, blithely making life or death decisions about living beings, moving earth from here to there, changing the course of waterways? The more one thinks about it, the odder it seems; this compulsion to remake a little corner of the planet according to some plan or vision.

Abby Adams, *What is a Garden Anyway*

ARTISTS' GARDENS

Building a garden in shingle on the salt-drenched, wind-exposed Suffolk coast, in the shadow of Dungeness nuclear power station, would be hard work for most gardeners. But it was a challenge that dying film director Derek Jarman embraced. And the result – buried sculptures of driftwood, rusty metal and beaten stones, unusually planted with marigolds and irises among the sea kale – has become a cult in its own right, attracting thousands of visitors every year.

UNUSUAL PLANTERS

Generations of gardeners have recycled worn-out old boots, shapeless hats and burnt saucepans to make unusual plant pots. But here are a few more unusual objects that have found their way into the garden:

A washing machine drum planted with melampodiums

A worn out silk purse planted with lamb's ears

An antique coal stove planted with hostas

A plastic snow sled planted with carnivorous bog plants

An old umbrella frame planted with sempervivum

A pair of jeans discarded and planted to celebrate the end of a successful diet and a life of gardening eased by the loss of 20lb.

QUOTE UNQUOTE

Keep a green tree in your heart and perhaps a singing bird will come.
CHINESE PROVERB

ON THE GRAPEVINE

We are probably all a little cranky in our ideas on manuring. The young man who used to collect the contents from his friends' ashtrays for later application to his roses is a case in point. Tea leaves get saved exclusively as a mulch for camellias, simply because the tea plant is a camellia species. For my part, I cast all my nail parings out of the bathroom window so as to feed the ceanothus below with hoof and horn. Since, at 30 years, this is the oldest ceanothus in my garden, and it is still flourishing, I naturally congratulate myself on a sagacious policy.
Christopher Lloyd, *The Well-Tempered Garden*

A VERY KEEN PUMPKIN

The world record for the largest pumpkin ever grown is
1,131lb. That's equivalent to the average weight of
TEN 13-year-old boys!

GARDEN COLLECTIVES

If you've ever been outwitted in the science and nature section of
Trivial Pursuit because you didn't know the collective name for a
group of porcupines (it is, funnily enough, 'a prickle'), then these
proper terms should come in handy. They are thought to have
originated in the 15th century and were first listed in the *Book of St
Albans* (Dame Juliana Barnes, 1486).

A **cete** of badgers
A **drift** of bees
A **dissimulation** of small birds
A **peep** of chickens
A **piteousness** of doves
A **raft** of ducks on water
A **business** of ferrets
A **charm** of finches
A **cloud** of flies
A **skulk** of foxes
A **kindle** of kittens
A **tiding** of magpies
A **richesse** of martins
A **labour** of moles
A **kit** of pigeons
A **flight** of swallows
A **wedge** of swans
A **herd** of wrens

ON THE GRAPEVINE

Cordelia: Alack! 'tis he: why, he was met even now
As mad as the vex'd sea; singing aloud;
Crown'd with rank fumiter and furrow weeds,
With burdocks, hemlock, nettles, cuckoo-flowers,
Darnel, and all the idle weeds that grow
In our sustaining corn. A century send forth;
Search every acre in the high-grown field,
And bring him to our eye.
                    William Shakespeare, *King Lear, Act IV, Scene 6*

In the search for wartime manure, keen gardeners would drive around the country with a bucket and spade in the back of their car and stop on the side of the road to scoop up any deposits thoughtfully left by a passing animal. Those living in the cities were less fortunate, although as the list below from *Gardening in War Time* (E Graham, 1940) shows, there was plenty else that could be put on the garden.

Horse manure is a dry, hot manure that warms up the soil. It is best applied to all crops in autumn, winter and spring.

Cow and pig manures are cold manures and best for use on light or medium soils. They are best applied in spring.

Decaying fish is a very effective manure, but it should be dug into the ground immediately, or heaped up and covered with earth, to avoid unpleasant smells.

Dried blood contains nitrogen in a form which is readily available to plants. It is best applied to the surface of the soil in solid form in spring or dissolved in water at the rate of 0.5oz to the gallon and applied weekly as a stimulant.

Flue dust is best applied to chalky soil in winter, as it increases its moisture-retaining power.

Fruit refuse can be piled up or dug into the soil and allowed to decay.

Goat and rabbit manures are good all-round fertilisers – not so rich in plant food but long lasting. They are best applied in winter in a heavy dressing.

Leather parings and dust are very slow-acting manures, that are best mixed with soil and kept soaked with household 'slop' for some months.

One of the richest of all manures is **night soil.** It is excellent for almost all garden purposes and suitable to all soils. Mix it with an equal quantity of earth and sprinkle with gypsum. This prevents the ammonia evaporating and acts as a deodoriser.

Seaweed is rich in potash and can either be burned or stacked in a heap and allowed to rot down before applying to the soil.

Sludge from a sewage precipitation plant is a good manure, best dusted with lime and applied in winter.

Keeping a small flock of laying **hens** will guarantee a constant supply of fine manures, self-applied.

Soot is an effective manure which also acts as a deterrent to insect pests and can be applied to soil straight from the chimney.

CULTURE VULTURE

Apiculture ....bee breeding for honey, beeswax or royal jelly
Arboriculture...........................the cultivation of trees and shrubs for ornamental or scientific purposes
Permaculture ....an ecologically-friendly system of gardening and agriculture
Silviculture............the commercial cultivation of trees and woodland
Sericulture ....silkworm breeding on mulberry trees for raw silk
Vermiculture........the farming of earthworms for compost or fishing
Viniculture........................the cultivation of grapes for wine-making
Floriculture ....the cultivation of flowering plants
Horticulture ....the cultivation of plants
Pomiculture ....the cultivation of fruit
Citriculture ....the cultivation of citrus fruits
Olericulture ....the cultivation of vegetables

QUOTE UNQUOTE

Just one word to smallholders, allotment holders and those who have a reasonable-sized garden – to those also who may be termed 'back-yarders'. You can help to feed yourselves and others... I ask for the fullest co-operation between all... The results of your work are of vital national importance.
Message from the Ministry of Agriculture to British citizens to do their bit during World War II

ANCIENT SEEDS

At least 300 million years old, cycads are one of the earth's oldest plants. Known for their large attractive palm-like leaves, there are about 300 different species and sub-species of cycads in Asia, Africa, the Americas and Australia, but an astonishing 53% of them are threatened with extinction. One of the problems is that these plants grow very slowly and depend on specialist pollinators. In one subspecies, the plants' natural pollinator no longer exists and pollination is done artificially.

They are suffering from habitat destruction, urban development, invasive plant species and collection for horticulture and landscaping. To discourage their collection from the wild, scientists have developed a unique method to tell if the cycads available for the garden are wild or cultivated using microchips and DNA-tracing techniques.

60 *Number, in thousands of tonnes, of nettles that were harvested by the Germans to make uniforms in World War I*

First created in 1965 for French television by Serge Danot, when it was called *Le Manège Enchanté*, *The Magic Roundabout* was bought by the BBC and given to Play School presenter Eric Thompson (father of actress, Emma Thompson) to translate. Eric decided that rather than translate the original scripts, he'd make up his own story-lines to fit the pictures and a cult television show was born.

With a five-minute slot just before the early evening news, *The Magic Roundabout* proved highly popular viewing, notching up a junior (and adult) audience of over eight million.

The show, which sent genera-tions to their pyjamas with Zebedee's standard declaration 'Time for bed', was set in a flower-power style garden with blue trees, pink mushrooms and big friendly flowers and even had its own gardener, Mr MacHenry who rode around on a tricycle.

Other cast members were Brian, the talkative snail, Dougal, the famously rude shaggy dog who lived on a strict diet of sugar, Dylan, the spaced-out rabbit, Ermintrude, the comtemplative, pink cow, Florence, the prim little girl and Zebedee, the jack-in-the-box type who bounced across the set.

The Magic Roundabout has been translated into 28 languages and has appeared on 98 television stations, and there is now *The Magic Roundabout Movie*, directed by Frank Passingham, with Jim Broadbent as the voice of Brian, Joanna Lumley as the voice of Ermintrude, Kylie Minogue as the voice of Florence, Richard O'Brien as the voice of Zebedee and Robbie Williams as the voice of Dougal.

A GARDEN WHODUNNIT

Who designed Agatha Christie's famous garden at Greenway in Devon? The National Trust, which possesses 300 acres of the crime and suspense writer's garden, are investigating the mystery. It is thought that Greenway was originally laid out by prisoners of war from the Spanish Armada, but the gardens were transformed in the 1790s and the Trust now suspects that garden designer Sir Humphrey Repton is responsible. Famed for his work at Woburn Abbey, Bloomsbury Square and Longleat, a typical Reptonian garden includes a terrace near the house and a serpentine park looked over by a distant view, and Greenway certainly seems to fit the brief.

Number of plants in the UK that are so rare, they are protected by law 61

Harris asked me if I'd ever been in the maze at Hampton Court. He said he went in once to show somebody else the way. He had studied it on a map, and it was so simple that it seemed foolish – hardly worth the two pence charged for admission. He said 'We'll just go in here, so that you can say you've been, but it's very simple. It's absurd to call it a maze. You keep on taking the first turning to the right. We'll just walk round for ten minutes and then go and get some lunch.'

They met some people soon after they had got inside, who said they'd been there for three quarters of an hour, and had had about enough of it. Harris told them they could follow him if they liked; he was just going in, and then would turn round and go out again. They said it was very kind of him, and fell behind and followed.

They picked up various other people who wanted to get it over as they went along, until they absorbed all the persons in the maze. People who had given up all hopes of ever getting in or out, or of ever seeing their home and friends again, plucked up their courage at the sight of Harris and his party, and joined the procession, blessing him... Harris kept on turning to the right, but it seemed a long way, and his cousin said he supposed it was a very big maze.

'Oh, one of the largest in Europe,' said Harris.

'Yes, it must be,' replied the cousin, 'because we've walked a good two miles already.'

Jerome K Jerome, *Three Men in a Boat*

LONDON'S SECRET GARDENS

Tucked in a quiet corner off Russell Square, above the School of Oriental and African Studies' Brunei Gallery can be found a Japanese roof terrace garden. Opened in November 2001, the garden, representing forgiveness, is designed with an area of raked sand, a checker board of pebbles and lemon thyme and a small stage – the perfect setting for Noh theatre.

KING SIZE WHEELBARROWS

The Chinese general, Chuko Liang, invented the wheelbarrow in 231 AD to enable his troops to move their supplies through mucky soil. His version was somewhat larger than the wheelbarrows we trundle around our gardens today, with a large front central wheel, backed by at least two rear wheels, and a big barrow flanked on either side by smaller good-holding boxes – definitely a two-person affair.

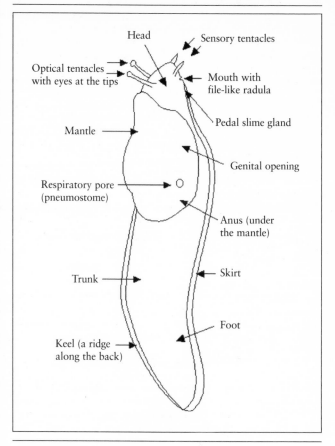

Head

Sensory tentacles

Optical tentacles with eyes at the tips

Mouth with file-like radula

Pedal slime gland

Mantle

Genital opening

Respiratory pore (pneumostome)

Anus (under the mantle)

Trunk

Skirt

Foot

Keel (a ridge along the back)

KEY TO THE MAZE

The Pineapple Garden Maze at Dole Plantation in Hawaii is officially recognised as the largest maze in the world. Covering an area of more than two acres, its paths last for nearly two miles and its grid is formed by more than 11,400 plants, including hibiscus, the official state flower of Hawaii.
To solve you must apparently turn L, R, R, L, but success cannot be guaranteed.

THE MEANING OF LIFF

In *The Meaning of Liff*, Douglas Adams and John Lloyd identified hundreds of common experiences, feelings, situations and even objects which we all know and recognise, but for which no word exists. They matched these up with the thousands of words which, in their opinion did nothing but loaf around on signposts pointing at places, thereby earning a place in everyday conversation and making a worthwhile contribution to society. Gardening contributions include:

Abruzzo (n.) The worn patch of ground under a swing.

Ambleside (n.) The talk given about the facts of life by a father to his son whilst walking in the garden on a Sunday afternoon.

Breckles (n.) A disease of artificial plants.

Burwash (n.) The pleasurable cool slosh of puddle water over the toes of your gumboots.

Haxby (n.) A garden implement found in a potting shed whose exact purpose is unclear.

Lutton Gowts (n.) The opposite of green fingers – the effortless propensity to cause plant death.

Poffley End (n.) The green bit of a carrot.

Todber (n.) One whose idea of a good time is to stand behind his front hedge and give surly nods to people he doesn't know.

Trispen (n.) A form of intelligent grass. It grows a single, tough stalk and makes its home on lawns. When it sees the lawnmower coming it lies down and pops up again after it has gone by.

BLOOMING PUZZLES

A fruity anagram
MOLGOOTPIS
Answer on page 153

AND WHAT DO YOU DO?

More than 8,000 guests at a royal garden party in Buckingham Palace in 2003 were stunned when a 17-year-old guest removed his clothes and approached the Queen after a £100 bet with his brother. Beefeaters quickly stepped in, tackled him to the ground and dragged him away. Commenting on the event, fellow guest and Liberal MP, Lembit Opik observed: 'I feel he showed a naked loyalty to the Queen. I applaud him.'

BEE CAREFUL

Different species of bumble-bees have different shaped tongues (nature's way of fitting them into the wide variety of flowers they pollinate), but as some species of flowers are becoming rarer, the bees that pollinate them are also dwindling in numbers:

Short-haired bumble-bee (*Bombus subterraneus*)
Declared extinct in the UK, this species was exported to New Zealand and could be introduced back into the UK, if it was judged it could survive.

Great yellow bumble-bee (*Bombus distinguendus*)
Extinct in England, there has been a 50% decline in Scotland since 1950. To encourage this bee into your garden, plant clover and common knapweed.

Shrill carder bee (*Bombus silvarum*)
There has been a 95% decline in England since 1960. To encourage this bee into your garden, plant tall grasses, thistles and knapweeds.

Large garden bumble-bee (*Bombus ruderatus*)
There has been a 95% decline in England since 1960 and this bee is thought to be on the verge of extinction. It has a very long tongue to get pollen out of deep flowered plants. To encourage this bee in the garden, grow comfrey and trefoil plants.

Humble carder bee (*Bombus humilis*)
There has been a 50% decline in England since 1950. To encourage this bee into your garden, plant plenty of aromatic shrubs and herbs such as lavender and mint as well as beans, peas and clover.

The decrease in the bumble-bee's wild habitat, brought about by intensive farming, and the drastic decline in insect pollinated plants in the garden (which many gardeners have abandoned in favour of sterile modern hybrids) are also responsible for the dropping population. To join in the fight to save the bumble-bee, opt for pollen-producing plants that attract bees and limit the number of hybrids in your garden.

ANIMALS – A DUTY TO FENCE

There is no general obligation on the garden owner to fence his land even when the garden is next to the public highway, but if he has animals on the garden, then he must fence to prevent the escape of animals onto the public highway. The Highway Authority can come onto your land and fence it off to protect the public. If your animals stray either onto the highway or a neighbouring owner's land, then you could be responsible for the damage that they cause.

AN EXPLOSIVE SUMMER

Some recent finds in British gardens

In June 2003, the Taylor family, who had just moved into their new house in Suffolk, were ordered not to go into their garden after they accidentally dug up two live shells. Police removed the shells, which are thought to have been aircraft shells from World War II.

A number of houses were evacuated in July 2003 after a man was shocked to discover a rusty shell sticking out of the earth in his garden in Tatsfield, Surrey. Bomb disposal experts relocated the shell to a safe place nearby for a controlled explosion.

In September 2003, a six-inch pet tarantula named Incey disappeared from his garden in Newport after his owner took him out for a stroll. Incey crawled off enthusiastically in the direction of a neighbouring garden and then, to the consternation of locals, vanished. But after a nerve-racking 17-hour search, little Incey, who had had her poisonous fangs removed, was discovered under a log and promptly returned to her cage.

In August 2003, a number of homes in Bath Road, Bristol were evacuated after a man dug up some containers full of a suspicious white powder, one of which was marked anthrax. Police closed off nearby roads while the substance was removed, but it was later found to be harmless.

And in September 2002, a boa constrictor was found hanging from a tree in a garden in Devon after being abandoned. RSPCA officers unwound the snake and put it into a duvet cover, before carrying it off to a local animal clinic. Wildlife liaison officers take a dim view of dumping non-indigenous pets in the wild, an offence that carries a two-year sentence.

ON THE GRAPEVINE

The rabbit has a charming face:
Its private life is a disgrace
I really dare not name to you
The awful things that rabbits do
Things that your paper never prints
You only mention them in hints.
They have such lost, degraded souls
No wonder they inhabit holes;
When such depravity is found
It only can live underground

Anon, *The Rabbit*

HERBAL SUBSTITUTES

If a recipe calls for a particular herb you haven't got in the garden,
try substituting it with one of these:

Basil ....oregano or thyme
Chervil ....tarragon or parsley
Chive...green onion, onion, or leek
Coriander ....parsley
Marjoram...basil, savoury or thyme
Mint..basil, marjoram or rosemary
Oregano ....thyme or basil
Parsley..chervil or coriander
Rosemary... thyme, tarragon or savoury
Sage ....savoury, marjoram or rosemary
Savoury ....thyme, marjoram or sage
Tarragon ....chervil, fennel seed or aniseed
Thyme ....basil, marjoram or oregano

QUOTE UNQUOTE

*He that planteth a tree is a servant of God, he provideth a kindness
for many generations, and faces that he hath not seen shall bless him.*
HENRY VAN DYKE, US poet and novelist

THE SAVAGE GARDEN

In Shakespeare's *Hamlet*, Claudius killed Hamlet's father with
henbane, a poisonous plant from the nightshade family.
According to the ghost of old Hamlet (Act 1, scene 5), it was a vile
death:

Sleeping within mine orchard,
My custom always in the afternoon,
Upon my secure hour thy uncle stole
With juice of cursed hebenon in a vial,
And in the porches of mine ears did pour
The leperous distilment; whose effect
Holds such an enmity with blood of man,
That, swift as quicksilver, it courses through
The natural gates and alleys of the body;
And with a sudden vigour it doth posset
And curd, like eager droppings into milk,
The thin and wholesome blood: so did it mine;
And a most instant tetter bark'd about,
Most lazar-like, with vile and loathsome crust,
All smooth body.

The number of Huernia varieties, succulents renowned for star-shaped 67
leaves, that smell like carrion

PENSÉE

C. de GONET, Editeur

In *Les Fleurs Animées*, JJ Grandville's paintings depict women adorned with bonnets, bodices and ribbons, each inspired by the flower she represents and a demeanour influenced by the language of flowers. In this case, a pansy for *pensée* (thoughts).

GREEN, AND CLEAN

Soaps were first developed 5,000 years ago – not for cleaning the body (that didn't come until later) but for cleaning cloth and wool. The first soaps are thought to have been made from wood ash and animal fat, and the world's oldest soap factory was discovered well-preserved under the lava and ash that wiped out Pompeii in 79 AD. Other early centres for soap making include Marseilles, Savona and Castille where soap was made from olive oil. As soap-making developed, different mixtures of plant oils, herbs and spices were used, including seaweed, honey, raisins and almonds. But soap was, until the industrial revolution, prohibitively expensive – well beyond the reaches of any but the richest classes. What changed this situation? The discovery that soap could be made from common salt, and the mass production methods that this discovery enabled, together with rising wages during the industrial revolution.

QUOTE UNQUOTE

Gardens are not made by sitting in the shade.
RUDYARD KIPLING, author

GARDEN SAINTS

Saint	Protector of
Dorothy	orchards and fruit tree growers
Antonio Abad	digging, tree holes and graves
Ysidro-Isadore	farmers, large gardens and shepherds
Francis of Assisi	garden birds, animals and ecology
Andreas	aquatic gardens, koi and goldfish
Barbara	lightning strikes and soil trouble-shooter
Bernardo Abad	beekeepers, flowers and vegetables
Antonio de Padua	lost items – such as small garden tools
Urban	vineyards and wine growers
Fiacre	herbs, vegetable gardens and male gardeners
Phocas	flower and ornamental gardening
Virgin Maria	garden sculptures
Valentine	lovers, and small, intimate, romantic gardens
Patrick	organic gardens
Adelard	gardeners
Elizabeth of Hungary	rose gardens and rose gardeners
Teresa Lisieux	florists
George	farmers
Ansovinus	crops
Virgin de Zapopan	plants from drought
Werenfried	vegetable gardens

HUCKLEBERRY THINGS

Huckleberries grow in the wild in north-west America. Although they are made into jams, jellies, wine, sweets and shampoos, huckleberries inspire a special mystique because man has not yet succeeded in cultivating them – partly because they only grow in areas above 4,000ft. Long prized by Indians, settlers to the north-west region immediately developed a taste for the fruit, which recently became the state fruit of Idaho. In the early 1800s, a huckleberry became a term for something that was small, unimportant and humble. Huckleberry Finn was so named by Mark Twain to indicate his low social status in the novel *Tom Sawyer*. Later, the expression 'I'm your huckleberry' became a term of affection for a friend or sweetheart and in the late 1950s, *Huckleberry Hound* was a popular cartoon about a blue dog who found life difficult to cope with.

BLOOMING PUZZLES

My first is in ocean but not in sea,
My second's in wasp but not in bee.
My third is in glider and also in flight,
My whole is a creature which comes out at night.
What am I?
Answer on page 153

GNOME GNOTES

Gnome fanciers in Amber Valley, Derbyshire were given an unwelcome Christmas present in December 2003 when they received official-looking letters stating their garden gnomes contravened planning laws and demanding the diminutive fellows be removed. When further investigation showed the letters to be a hoax, owners were told by the local council to ignore them.

ENTOMO-LOGIC

Proverbs are like butterflies, some are caught and some fly away
When spiders unite, they can tie down a lion
Never look for a worm in the apple of your eye
A hive of bees in May is worth a load of hay
A closed mouth catches no flies
A louse in the cabbage is better than no meat at all
It is not summer until the crickets sing
Laws catch flies, but let hornets go free

CRUISING IN THE GARDEN

Some public gardens and parks have earned less wholesome reputations as areas where people have met, not for a walk round the tulip beds, or a cup of tea by the pond, but a secret assignation in the bushes.

Certain gardens are particularly popular gay cruising locations – such as Bloomsbury Garden (before it was closed for renovation) and a number of other central London parks and gardens. Hampstead Heath, London's most famous cruising ground, has apparently seen rustling in its bushes for over 200 years. Since local police admit they only have three officers to patrol the 700-acre site, all of whom clock off at 10pm, the chances are that cruising in this particular park is likely to continue unabated for another 200.

Celebrities, however, cruise at their peril. In 1998, George Michael was arrested for lewd behaviour after an undercover officer caught him one-handed in the men's toilet of a Beverly Hills Park. Michael's popularity survived the crisis of his arrest, his gay outing, and the psychological counselling he was ordered to seek, and he released *Outside*, a single accompanied by a video of dancing policemen set in a public toilet.

Cruising is not unheard of among politicians either. In 1998, Welsh Secretary and Labour MP, Ron Davies resigned over his role in that famous Clapham Common incident.

But Ron has not been the only ministerial cruiser. In 1958, Tory Ian Harvey was arrested with a Coldstream guardsman after a policeman heard rustling in a bush in St James's Park and decided to investigate. The Minister attempted to make a run for it, but failed, then gave a false name at the police station and was charged with gross indecency and a breach of the park's regulations.

When the case reached court the charge of indecency was dropped and both parties were fined £5. Like Davies however, Harvey found himself cast out in the political wilderness and shunned by members of his party.

A PINTLE FOR THE LADIES

In some parts of England, arum lilies used to be known as cuckoo's pintles – perhaps because of the flower's somewhat suggestive shape – as a pintle was a colloquial name for a penis. Before going out for an evening, some young men would place a cuckoo's pintle in their shoe after the saying: 'I place you in my shoe, let all girls be drawn to you.'

THE KEENEST ROYAL
GARDENER OF THEM ALL

The keenest gardener among the current Royal Family is Prince Charles. His interest developed when he acquired Highgrove, an 18th century country mansion in Gloucestershire. A beginner himself, with a reputation for conversing with his plants, the Prince assembled an impeccable team of advisers to assist. Reputed to have spent £500,000 restoring the gardens, Highgrove is now a showcase for traditional and organic growing methods.

Yew hedges were planted around the house and the traditional rose garden for privacy. Wildflower lawns now lead up to the house and in spring, a regal green carpet is mowed through the centre to show off the thousands of tulips on either side.

Not content with pleasing the eye aesthetically, Prince Charles is also a leading advocate of the environmental movement and, where his own garden is concerned, he puts his vast sums of money where his organic mouth is. No pesticides, weedkillers or artificial fertilisers are used on his estate. The ground benefits from compost made by recycling garden rubbish. There's even a reed-bed sewage treatment plant, which according to reports filters princely deposits into a pool so pure it is frequented by royal kingfishers and dragonflies – apparently a sign of good water quality.

The garden isn't open to the public but the Prince does host various functions there for his different charitable concerns. If you're not likely to receive an invite to one of them, you might be able to get on one of his organised tours by applying in writing to St James's Palace. Be prepared to wait though – at the moment there's a waiting list of up to five years.

GARDEN SPEAK

Gardening is an occupation pursued by thousands around the galaxy. Here are the names for garden in seven other languages:

Word	Language	Spoken in
a-du-s-gi	Cherokee	USA (American Indian)
vaj (lub)	Hmong	Laos
igadi	Xhosa	Southern Africa
bustani	Swahili	Eastern Africa
senzai	Japanese	Japan
hardin	Ilongo	Philippines
wIjghachHom	Klingon	Star Trek

Number, in thousands, of four leaf clover leaves that George Kaminski has collected from the gardens of his prison in Pennsylvania

THE GRASS PRETENDERS

There are some 9,000 species of grass in the world, but these plants, called grass, are not among them:

China grass or remie or rhea (*Boehmeria nivea*) is a nettle grown for bast fibres from the *Urticaceae* family.

Ditch grass or widgeon grass (*Ruppia maritima*) is actually a vascular plant that prefers growing in wetlands.

Fish grass (*Cabomba caroliniana*) is, as you might expect, a plant that grows in water.

Mondo grass or lily turf (*Ophiopogon japonicus*) looks little like grass, with white flowers and red berries.

Nut grass is a common lawn pest (*Cyperus rotundus)* and actually a weed – a lawn invader which takes over and is hard to get rid of.

Pepper grass (*Lipidium spp.*) is edible, and also known as curly cress.

Saw grass (*Cladium jamaicense)* is abundant in sub-tropical marshlands and has fine serrated leaves.

Scurvy grass (*Oxalis enneaphylla*) has thick flat leaves, pink or white flowers and apparently provides relief for ulcers.

Seagrasses, *(Vallisneria americana)*, including eel grass, are aquatic plants that have ribbon-like leaves.

Sleeping grass (*Mimosa pudica*) is a spiky legume that can grow to six feet, with leaves that droop when touched but recover after a few minutes.

CELEBRITY GARDENERS

Percy Thrower started off the whole cult of celebrity gardening in 1956 when he presented a monthly gardening programme called *Gardening Club*. The very image of a cardigan-wearing old codger who fiddled around the potting shed, Percy presented at a time when open-air filming was a laborious and complicated affair, and so that he could be heard, microphones were buried into the soil around the TV gardens – the system revealed its glitch, the day Percy decided to do a spot of watering!

Percy went on to appear in children's favourite *Blue Peter,* and present *Gardeners' World*, but left the BBC in disgrace after appearing in an advert on a rival channel. He continued to be an active celebrity gardener and won a number of honours, including an MBE, an appearance on *This is Your Life* and perhaps the highest, most lasting honour of all: the naming of numerous hybrids after him.

PLANTS AND SEX AND ROCK AND ROLL

If the rose symbolises love, the lily purity, and the bluebell consistency, then the orchid can mean only one thing – sex.

At least that's what the prudish Victorians thought. They restricted the women of the age from growing the blooms for fear the flowers were too sexually suggestive. But then, even the father of botany, Theophrastus found the spherical tubers a little on the erotic side; it is he that first named them *orkhis*, which is derived from the Greek for testicle.

Only Queen Victoria was able to pursue her passion for orchids with success – largely because she appointed a well-known collector to the court in the position of Royal Orchid Grower.

Ordinary women, however, got their own back – if not on the men, but certainly on the orchids. In 1912, suffragettes managed to destroy almost the entire collection of orchids at Kew Gardens.

QUOTE UNQUOTE

To create a little flower is the labour of ages.
WILLIAM BLAKE, poet

BLOOMING PUZZLES

I am a house, hidden from view
I am built throughout without nails or glue
I exist to hold pale gems of blue
So look up above if you need a clue
What am I?
Answer on Page 153

FACTS ABOUT FUNGI

Fungi do not contain chlorophyll, the green pigment by which plants synthesise the sun's energy, and therefore aren't really plants at all. They get their nutrients from living organisms, plants and animals and decaying organic matter by assisting in the decomposition process. Many fungi are beneficial, such as the penicillin-producing *Penicillium notatum*, and others are destructive, such as the *Ophiostoma* carried by beetles which causes dutch elm disease. Others are edible, such as the *Lactobacillus* that turns milk into yoghurt and the *Saccharomyces cereviceae*, also known as yeast.

The number of acres contained in this garden was such as Catherine could not listen to without dismay, being more than double the extent of all Mr. Allen's, as well her father's, including church-yard and orchard. The walls seemed countless in number, endless in length; a village of hot-houses seemed to arise among them, and a whole parish to be at work within the enclosure. The general was flattered by her looks of surprise, which told him almost as plainly, as he soon forced her to tell him in words, that she had never seen any gardens at all equal to them before; and he then modestly owned that, 'without any ambition of that sort himself – without any solicitude about it – he did believe them to be unrivalled in the kingdom. If he had a hobby-horse, it was that. He loved a garden. Though careless enough in most matters of eating, he loved good fruit – or if he did not, his friends and children did. There were great vexations, however, attending such a garden as his. The utmost care could not always secure the most valuable fruits. The pinery had yielded only one hundred in the last year. Mr. Allen, he supposed, must feel these inconveniences as well as himself.'

'No, not at all. Mr. Allen did not care about the garden, and never went into it.'

With a triumphant smile of self-satisfaction, the general wished he could do the same, for he never entered his, without being vexed in some way or other, by its falling short of his plan.

Jane Austen, Northanger Abbey

MIDDLE STUMPS AND TREE STUMPS

Many young cricketing hopefuls up and down the country practise their skills in the garden. Here's an England XI that never left it:

G Bean	1891/2
R Berry	1950
MC Bird	1909/10–1913/14
W Flowers	1884/5–1893
WE Hollies	1934/5–1950
AA Lilley	1896–1903/4
AE Moss	1953/4–1960
E Peate	1881/2–1886
CF Root	1926
BC Rose	1977/8–1980
J Vine	1911/2

In July 1917, 16-year-old Elsie Wright went down into the bottom of her garden with her 10-year-old cousin Francis Griffiths and her father's camera. When her father developed the film, he discovered a picture of Francis with five fairies and Elsie with a gnome. The family regarded the pictures as a joke until 1919, when Frances' mother mentioned them at a theosophists' meeting in Bradford. They immediately attracted attention, and before long the eminent theosophist, Edwin Gardner declared them to be real.

The photos were taken at the height of 'spirit photography', a craze which saw photographers make vast sums by seemingly photographing the ghost of a dead relative, secure in the knowledge that few knew how the camera worked. Gardner wasn't the only one to fall for the tricks, many contemporaries also believed that the camera could see what the human eye could not.

In June 1920, Sir Arthur Conan Doyle got in on the act. He published copies of the photos in *Strand Magazine* and sent his friend Geoffrey Hodson up to Cottingley where the girls lived to see if he could find the fairies in the the garden. Conan Doyle's subsequent article, which claimed the photos were genuine, attracted hundreds of letters from readers who claimed they had also seen fairies in the garden. But the creator of Sherlock Holmes was not believed by all, and he provoked further ridicule with the publication of a book on the Cottingley fairies – leading some to question his mental state.

It was not for another 65 years, when a writer discovered almost identical pictures of the 'fairies' in a children's anthology that the girls were exposed. In an interview in *The Times* in 1983, Elsie admitted the fairies were fakes that had been copied from the anthology, mounted on cardboard and stuck in bushes with hat pins. Conan Doyle, it now appears, had been well and truly fooled, and deserving of JE Wheelwright's scorn:

If you, Sir Conan Doyle, believe in fairies,
Must I believe in Mister Sherlock Holmes?
If you believe that round us all the air is
Just thick with elves and little men and gnomes,
Then must I now believe in Doctor Watson
And speckled bands and things?
Oh, no! My hat!
Though all the t's are crossed and i's have dots on
I simply can't Sir Conan. So that's that!

BACK FROM THE BRINK

When a Wollemi pine was discovered in an isolated grove in Australia in 1994, it caused something of a scientific sensation. The species, which is believed to be more than 200 million years old, was thought to have become extinct two million years ago, and its only previous traces had been fossilised remains.

For 10 years, the Australian government kept the 'dinosaur tree' a closely guarded secret and initiated a breeding programme to promote its cultivation. In true *X-files* style, scientists flown to the site were blindfolded to prevent them from betraying the tree's location, and seeds from the tip of the pine were collected by dangling from a helicopter. Thankfully a more effective method has since been discovered (involving catching the seeds in nets) and the pines will soon be available to grow in gardens. This is good news for British gardeners; the trees thrive in cold climates and low light.

WHAT'S IN A BOY'S NAME?

Aiken	Made of oak
Arthur	Stone or rock
Ashley	Ash trees
Bruce	Copse or small wood
Evelyn	Hazel nut
Janus	Gateway
Laurence	Laurel
Lee	Wood, clearing or meadow
Lindsey	Linden tree
Ogden	Valley of oaks
Sherlock	Area of land
Sylvester	Wood
Vernon	Springtime or alder tree
Stanley	Stony meadow

LONDON'S SECRET GARDENS

What a place to give birth in! Hidden away on the seventh floor of St Thomas's Hospital is a tranquil indoor garden that was designed as a quiet place to help mothers-to-be in the early stages of labour. With inspiring views of the Thames and Big Ben, the garden is designed with silk and real foliage, and mothers-to-be have reported an increase in the ease of childbirth.

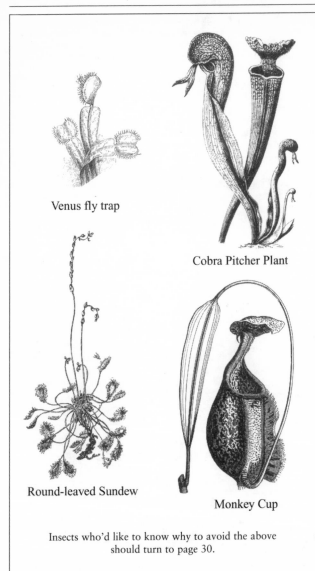

Venus fly trap

Cobra Pitcher Plant

Round-leaved Sundew

Monkey Cup

Insects who'd like to know why to avoid the above

NEIGHBOURLY NEGLIGENCE

Like branches, roots that grow from your land onto a neighbour's are trespassing. Your neighbour can chop the roots along the boundary line and they do not need your permission to do so. Your roots can substantially damage your neighbour's property by growing under the foundations of their house, making them unsafe, or drying the soil, resulting in subsidence. In these cases damages could include:

1. The cost of repairs.

2. The difference in the value of the house if it is sold at a loss.

3. Any other expenses arising from the trespass.

4. All legal costs.

5. The cost of a court order, and the cost of cutting back the branches or roots, or of cutting down the tree itself.

Subsidence or damage caused by tree roots which involves a claim, will generally be considered a nuisance rather than trespass if it has to go to court. Naturally a negotiated agreement with neighbours would be preferable and less costly.

NUDGE NUDGE, WINK WINK…IT'S A TOMATO

Tomatoes originated in South America. They were 'discovered' in 1550 by Spanish settlers in Mexico and brought back to Spain from where they quickly spread around Europe. In France, they became known as 'pomme d'amour' (apple of love) acquiring a risqué reputation as an aphrodisiac and in England, where they were also known as 'love apples', they were only grown as decorative plants that were whispered about.

ON THE GRAPEVINE

Iago: Virtue? a fig! 'Tis in ourselves that we are thus or thus. Our bodies are our gardens, to the which our wills are gardeners: so that if we will plant nettles, or sow lettuce, set hyssop and weed up thyme, supply it with one gender of herbs, or distract it with many, either to have it sterile with idleness, or manured with industry, why, the power and corrigible authority of this lies in our wills.
William Shakespeare, *Othello, The Moor of Venice, Act I, Scene 3*

Percentage of people who say they compost their organic kitchen and garden 79
waste according to a recent survey

SAY IT WITH FLOWERS

Do you speak flower? The custom of communicating by sending flowers is believed to have originated in Persia. It was later adopted in Turkey in the 18th century and became very popular in Europe in the 19th century when it was used by couples as a secret method of conveying messages. One of the most popular flower symbols was the rose (to denote love), but the way the flower was cut and presented also influenced the message conveyed:

A rosebud with leaves and thorns – I fear but I hope
The bud of a red rose – You are pure and lovely
A rose in full bloom placed over two buds – We must be secret
A cluster of musk roses – I think you are charming
A moss rose – Voluptuous love
A withered red rose – I would rather die for our love is over
A rugosa rose – Your only attraction is your beauty

QUOTE UNQUOTE

They kill good trees to put out bad newspapers.
JAMES G WATT, former US Secretary of the Interior

GARDEN GAGS

A man walks into a flower shop: 'I'd like some flowers please.'
'Certainly, sir. What did you have in mind?'
He shrugs: 'Well I'm not sure, I uh, I uh, I uh...'
'Perhaps I could help. What exactly have you done?'

GRASSED UP

1. A thickly planted lawn measuring about 10,000 square feet, will on average contain 8.5 million grass plants, with three billion miles of roots to support it. That's the equivalent of 15 return trips to the sun.

2. By weight, grass clippings are approximately 90% water.

3. Cats eat grass to aid their digestion and to help them get rid of any fur in their stomachs.

4. The natural yellow colour of butter comes mainly from beta-carotene found in the grass the cows graze on.

GNOME GNOTES

The shadowy French organisation, the Garden Gnome Liberation Front (GGLF) was formed to free gnomes (*nains de jardin*) from the tyranny of their slave-like existence in French gardens in 1997. Since then, the now worldwide GGLF has dedicated itself to the job of removing gnomes and 'de-ridiculising' them by placing them back in their natural environment. So far an estimated 6,000 of the little fellows have disappeared. Here are some of the top gnome breakouts:

- In 2001, the GGLF kidnapped 75 gnomes from the gardens of Saint-Die-des-Vosges near Strasbourg. Police searched for them without success until one Sunday morning, the little abductees were discovered lined up on the steps of the local cathedral as if they intended to go to Mass. Police then tried to reunite the gnomes with their owners on 'Gnome Return Day', but only 32 of the figures were collected.

- September 1998 saw a gnome suicide *en masse* – 11 were found hanging by their necks from a bridge in Briey, eastern France. A suicide note found nearby said: 'When you read these words, we will no longer be part of your selfish world, where we serve merely as decoration.'

- 1998 also saw a hundred-strong gnome demonstration in the centre of a roundabout in Chavelot. Local police compared the set-up to a 'giant creche'.

- In March 2000, the GGLF liberated 20 of the figures from a Paris 'Gnome Exhibition' in a night-time raid.

- In July 2000, the GGLF left hundreds on liberated gnomes on a football field in Les Deux-Sevres France.

And remember, if you do want to join in the fight, the GGLF recommend you lift from the knees and don't twist.

THE WORLD'S SMALLEST SEED

You may know orchids have tiny seeds, but did you know that the seed of a coral root orchid is so small, it is barely visible to the human eye? At no more than 0.2mm in diameter and weighing 35 millionths of an ounce, the seed is actually no larger than a fungal spore.

The seed is so small because it contains no food reserves. To grow, it must establish a symbiotic relationship with surrounding fungi. It absorbs carbohydrates and minerals from the fungus which, a fine middleman, in turn absorbs these nutrients from surrounding trees.

THE SHADOWY MARCH OF TIME

Sunshine or not, sundials, the earliest known form of time-keeping, have stood for centuries in grey and cloudy British gardens. But they started life around 2000 BC as simple poles, with the direction and length of the shadow giving an approximate time of day. The Greeks and Romans developed more sophisticated forms, placing vertical or horizontal 'gnomons' (the rod of the sundial that casts the shadow) into the hollow of a bowl marked with hour lines. It was not until the 1st century AD that it was demonstrated that a gnomon set parallel to the Earth's axis would cast a shadow in the same direction at the same time every day of the year.

In the 1930s, sundial fanatic Charles Boursier travelled round Europe, devotedly looking at the inscriptions on sundials, which he published in a collection titled *Devises de Cadrans Solaires*. Here are eight of the 800 inscriptions he collected:

Sol me probat unus ....Only the sun can prove that I am useful
Horas non numero nisi serenas ....I show only the bright hours
Tempus fugit ....Time flies
Lucem demonstrat umbra ....It is light that makes a shadow
Sol omnibus lucet ....The sun shines for all
Serius est quam cogitas ....It is later than you think
Vidi nihil permanere sub sole ....I have seen nothing last forever
under the sun
Meam vide umbram, tuam videbris vitam ....Look at my shadow,
you will see your life

GNOME GNOTES

How gnomes began, let alone why gardeners began fouling up their gardens with them, is vague. One has this nebulous notion that in some way, without quite knowing why, they're mixed up with leprechauns, the little people, the Brothers Grimm and Scandinavian wood-cutters, fertility symbols, and those seven dwarfs who stole all the scenes without much difficulty from that dreadful Snow White.

The fertility symbol theory, to which a lot of gnomers subscribe, seems especially dicey. For one thing, I don't know if you've noticed this, but all gnomes appear to be male. Naturally, a vast amount of research has been carried out before writing this chapter; not a gnome have I gnoted wearing high heels or carrying a handbag, not that carrying a handbag these days is any cast-iron criterion of gender. Yet there they all are, blissfully happy, grinning away, and not a dame in sight.

Alan Melville, *Gnomes and Gardens*

THE HIGH PRICE OF PEAT

Over 90% of Britain's peat bogs have been destroyed or irreparably damaged during the last 50 years, when peat-filled compost has become a popular option for gardening. Some peat bogs are thousands of years old, and very valuable to us as a source of knowledge about our past.

Seeds, plant remains, artifacts and even human remains have been found in peat bogs, including the aptly named Pete Marsh, the 2,300-year-old man who was discovered in peat bogs at Lindow Moss in 1983. Pete was unfortunately cut in half by a mechanical excavator when he was discovered.

He was apparently 25 years old when he was killed in a ritualised murder which involved bashing him round the head, strangling him with a rope and cutting his throat. Pete and other ancient remains found at the site, including the head of a woman, were moved to the British Museum for further investigation.

The woman was found to be very old indeed – dating back 2,000 years. This discovery came too late for a local man who, frantic from the fear of immediate discovery, confessed to murdering and burying his wife in the peat.

BLOOMING PUZZLES

Unravel the following phrase to make a flowery cliché
WE FLIRT SO THIS WAY
Answer on Page 153

POISONOUS PLANTS

In September 1978, exiled Bulgarian writer Georgi Markov was poisoned with a pellet of ricin, a deadly extract from the seed of the castor oil plant. The poor Markov was jabbed in the leg by an umbrella. Its owner apologised and walked away. Markov felt a stinging pain from the jab and when he got to work at the BBC World Service he noticed a tiny red pimple had formed on his leg. That evening he fell ill, and three days later, died. After his death, doctors found a small platinum pellet 1.5mm in diameter embedded in his calf which showed traces of ricin. The pellet was believed to have been injected through the tip of a KGB modified umbrella aimed at Markov's leg as he walked across Waterloo Bridge. The facts of the case were subsequently confirmed by KGB defector Oleg Gordievsky, although no one has ever been charged with the murder.

SQUIRRELED AWAY

Imagine taking the time and effort over Christmas to decorate your garden trees with 250 Christmas fairy lights, only to find that after two days they have all vanished. That's what happened to Sally Kennett's family in Swindon. But the bulbs were taken by no ordinary garden thief – they were stolen by a pack of squirrels, who chewed off the bulbs and then secreted them throughout the garden, presumably in preparation for their own Christmas lunch.

HOW TO WATER IN A SCORCHER?

With summers getting hotter and hotter, gardeners will be using more and more water to keep their cherished plants alive. But plants don't necessarily need to be drenched with a water guzzling hose, indeed some prefer to dry out. Here are a few tips to enable gardeners to save precious water without damaging their plants:

1. During a drought, lawns may dry out and turn brown, but this doesn't mean they have died. It would take eight months without rain for a lawn to wither away, which would be unlikely to happen in Britain's wet and windy winters. To keep a lawn looking good in a drought, leave it a little longer than normal by setting the mower at its highest setting.

2. Water the garden either early in the morning or late in the evening. This will prevent the water from evaporating before the roots get a good soaking and it will stop the leaves and flowers scorching under the water drops of the midday sun. You should also water infrequently. This will make plants more resilient and able to resist drought.

3. Choose plants that thrive in droughts, such as buddleia, jasmine, lavender, rosemary and sunflowers, and avoid water-loving plants like bamboo, clematis and azalea. Try to plant water-loving plants together so that water isn't wasted.

4. Collect rainwater using a water butt rather than using freshwater.

QUOTE UNQUOTE

We sow with all the art we know and not a plant appears.
A single seed from any weed a thousand children rears.
ANON

84 *Number, in thousands of people, who went to an accident and emergency department after an injury sustained in the garden in 1998*

PASSION PLAY

The three styles represent the nails that nailed Jesus to the cross

The passion flower's ovary represents the sponge soaked in vinegar

The five stamens represent Jesus's wounds

Leaf representing the spear with which Jesus was pierced

The crown representing Jesus's crown of thorns

Tendrils representing the lashes with which Jesus was beaten

Ten petals representing the ten faithful apostles, the unfaithful pair Judas Iscariot and Peter who denied knowing Jesus at his trial are not represented.

Since its introduction into Europe in the 17th century, the passion flower has been seen by Christians as a symbol of the crucifixion

IF YOU CAN'T BEAT THEM, EAT THEM

A good way of getting rid of weeds is to eat them. Check to make sure you can eat them before enthusiastically attacking your garden with a knife and fork. The following are not poisonous.

Latin name	Common name	Edible parts
Arctium spp.	Burdock	Root
Taraxacum officinale	Dandelion	Roots, leaves, flowers
Rumex crispus	Dock	Leaves
Rumex acetosella	Sheep sorrel	Leaves, seeds
Trifolium pratense	Shepherd's purse	Leaves, seeds
Rosa spp.	Wild rose	Petals

In the 1930s and 1940s, the back gardens of Hollywood were the private playpens of the stars. David Niven's autobiography *The Moon's A Balloon* uncovers some of the secrets:

On Douglas Fairbanks

Doug enjoyed hugely displaying his acrobatic talents and watching those half his age trying to catch up with him. I nearly killed myself jumping off his high-diving board on to the low spring-board alongside, which he had assured me would give a 'real tremendous bounce'. It did. I missed the water altogether and landed in some petunias below the drawing room window.

On Mike Todd

Mike Todd, always flamboyant, had steaks flown out from Kansas City on his private plane for a party of six, and proudly displayed them to Elizabeth Taylor, Eddie Fisher, Debbie Reynolds, Hjordis and myself. He was going to cook them a new way, he announced, and at his barbecue pit on a hillside he left them surrounded by sauces, oil and brushes, then he took us into the house to wait till his charcoal fire was perfect. A fox ate the steaks and Todd had to send out for Chinese food.

On Greta Garbo

I was afforded one more mini glimpse of the famous recluse when Edmund Golding, the director, invited me for a weekend at his desert retreat above Palm Springs. I arrived hot and dusty after a long drive and Golding pointed the way to his swimming pool in the palm trees below.

'Go and cool off,' he ordered.

As I neared the pool it became apparent that standing in the shallow end was a naked female figure. As this incident took place in the mid-thirties the reader will understand that I retreated to the house and asked my host to clarify the situation.

'Oh!' he said, 'it's only Garbo... she's staying somewhere down there and uses the pool when she feels like it.' I hastened once more down the garden path, but I was too late – all that remained was the disturbed surface of the water.

On Errol Flynn and John Huston

Flynn loved fighting: he took it seriously and kept himself in a permanent state of readiness at 601 North Linden. John Huston also liked a good punch up now and then. On one famous occasion he and Flynn decided that they were bored at a Hollywood soirée. 'Tell you what, Kid,' said Huston. 'Let's get the hell outta here and go down to the bottom of the garden and just mix it a little. Whaddya say?'

'You're on!' said Flynn... They both ended up in the Cedars of Lebanon Hospital for emergency repairs.

CYCLAMEN CALENDAR

Garden cyclamens are very useful little plants. Not only will they grow
under trees since they thrive in shade, each cyclamen corm will last a
very long time (possibly longer than their owner) and they seed
themselves. Clever planting will ensure cyclamens throughout the year:

Date	Cyclamen
Mid spring	*C. ibericum*
Mid spring	*C. repandum*
Late spring	*C. balearicum*
Summer	*C. europaeum*
Late summer	*C. purpurascens*
Autumn	*C. cilicium*
Late autumn	*C. neapolitanum*
Winter and spring	*C. coum*

ON THE GRAPEVINE

Every garden has its own particular feature, something unique, which
is its focus and its strength, and which gives it its character and distin-
guishes it from every other garden. It may be its situation or shape or a
certain aspect or vista within it, or else something individual – a tree or
shrub, unusual or fine, an archway, a gate, an old wall, a summer-
house, a perfect lawn. You have only to discover and recognise that
individuality, and allow it to express itself, or at least, do nothing to
destroy or detract from it. Like the charm of a person, it may not be
revealed to you at once, or even for a year or more, but if you live in
humble and expectant mood with a garden, in the course of time you
will come to know it. And if you begin with a bare and muddy acre,
unplanted, unshaped, then you can help to mould the character of the
garden to yourself.

Susan Hill, *Through the Garden Gate*

SAFFRON SUCCOTASH!

The spice saffron comes – surprise, surprise – from the saffron
crocus. Indeed the word crocus comes from the Greek word for
saffron – *krokos*. Few gardeners cultivate the saffron crocus, which
is a sorry looking plant that is prone to disease. Saffron is believed
to have been introduced into England by the Romans and by the
time of Henry VIII, it was being used to dye the royal sheets as an
antiseptic. In the 17th century, there was a great industry of saffron
at Saffron Walden, but much of today's saffron now comes from
Iran. Each saffron crocus has three stigmas and it takes about 4,400
stigmas to make an ounce of saffron.

CELEBRITY GARDENERS

Of all the celebrity gardeners, the late **Geoff Hamilton** is one of the most memorable. Geoff fronted *Gardeners' World* for more than 17 years. Born in Stepney in August 1936, Geoff's family moved to Broxborne in Hertfordshire and his passion with gardening began, shortly after he discovered the garden at the age of four. A trained horticulturist, Geoff started out as a freelance landscape designer, who wrote for the *Garden News* and *Practical Gardening* magazines. His first television job was *Gardening Diary* and from there he started appearing as a guest presenter on *Gardeners' World*. But *Gardeners' World* producers seemed strangely reluctant to make him a regular presenter, although he finally made it in 1979, swiftly finding a suitably large garden on which he could experiment – 'Barnsdale' was born and gardening history was made.

ON THE GRAPEVINE

From the orchard across the way the smell of ripe pears floats over the child's bed. A band rehearses waltzes in the distance. White things gleam in the dark – white flowers and paving stones. The moon on the window panes careens to the garden and ripples the succulent exhalations of the earth like a silver paddle. The world is younger than it is, and she to herself appears so old and wise, grasping her problems and wrestling with them as affairs peculiar to herself and not as racial heritages. There is a brightness and bloom over things; she inspects life proudly, as if she walked in a garden forced by herself to grow in the least hospitable of soils. She is already contemptuous of ordered planting, believing in the possibility of a wizard cultivator to bring forth sweet smelling blossoms from the hardest of rocks, and night-blooming vines from barren wastes, to plant the breath of twilight and to shop with marigolds. She wants life to be easy and full of pleasant reminiscences.

Zelda Fitzgerald, *Save me the Waltz*

BULLOCKS!

A topiary sculpture of a life-size longhorn bull which was installed in Fort Worth's Sundance Square left no part of its anatomy to the imagination. The US$4,000 Jasmine sculpture provoked so many amused comments of the 'he certainly has the right equipment' variety that after only two weeks the developers decided they'd had enough. Early one morning a surgical squad arrived and within a few minutes the once anatomically-correct bull was deprived of its most famous appendage.

---

88 *Percentage of 'green spaces' in Beira, Mozambique that are used for 'family agriculture'*

DUPED ON DOPE

When staff at the Conservative party's Welsh headquarters in Cardiff found some unexpected new visitors in the office's back garden in the summer of 2002, they thought they were tomato plants. With expectations of a bumper crop, they let them continue to grow until the gardener pointed out they were actually cultivating cannabis plants. At which point, and no doubt with a touch of embarrassment, they called in a constable.

It's not clear how the plants got there (a political prank by a determined rival?), but after further inquires, police decided a cheeky local had planted his own supply in the Tory party's back garden. They probably expected that they'd rest undiscovered among the overgrown weeds, but that even if they didn't, someone else would surely get the blame, and there'd be red faces all round.

FROSTY FRIENDS

Although frost is usually thought of as white crystals that form on the ground after a cold night, there are actually different types:

Air frost happens when the temperature just over a metre above the ground has fallen to zero, but the temperature on the ground is higher. Air frost usually happens in autumn when the soil temperatures are still high from the summer.

Ground frost occurs when the air temperature is above zero but the ground still reaches freezing point.

Hoar frost occurs when white crystals form on the ground on a cold morning. Hoar frost occurs when the air cools and water condenses onto the grass at below freezing point. Water that condenses on the grass above freezing point is dew.

Frozen dew is different from hoar frost – it is simply water that has condensed onto the grass above freezing point and subsequently frozen.

ADONIS GARDEN

An 'adonis garden' is an allusion for a worthless toy or something that is perishable. It comes from the ancient Greek practice of planting adonis gardens for the annual festival of young huntsmen. Adonis gardens consisted of lettuce and fennel, and they were thrown away on the morning following the festival.

DRIFTIN' ON AN OCEAN WAVE

Tropical drift seeds and drift fruits can survive for months and even years at sea. Their thick shells are impervious to sea water and each seed has a way of retaining buoyancy through internal air cavities that makes them capable of crossing large oceans. It is, however, a somewhat hit-and-miss dispersal method; many float for months over thousands of miles only to end up parched on a beach, or worse, float out of tropical waters into Europe where the climate is too cold for them to develop. Of the 250 or so species that commonly collect on tropical beaches, only half are able to float in seawater for more than a month and still be viable. The drift seeds that are brought to land by tsunamis (tidal waves) are the lucky ones; they are deposited high enough for them to germinate and develop.

In order to find out exactly how long it takes for seeds to drift across oceans, the US Coast and Geodetic Survey decided to do some experimenting. They put bottles into the sea containing numbered postcards, which requested the finders to fill out the cards and mail them back. Of their results, one bottle took about one year to drift from Yucatan to Ireland and another took four months to float from Caracas in Venezuela to Florida Keys in the US.

REASONS TO STAY OUT OF THE GARDEN

Herpetophobia	a fear of reptiles or creepy crawlies
Hygrophobia	a fear of damp
Kyphophobia	a fear of stooping
Lachanophobia	a fear of vegetables
Melissophobia	a fear of bees
Misophobia	a fear of being contaminated by germs or dirt
Mottephobia	a fear of moths
Mycophobia	a fear of mushrooms
Murophobia	a fear of mice
Nebulaphobia	a fear of fog
Nephophobia	a fear of clouds
Nyctohylophobia	a fear of dark wooded areas at night
Ornithophobia	a fear of birds
Pagophobia	a fear of ice or frost
Phyllophobia	a fear of leaves
Ranidaphobia	a fear of frogs
Rupophobia	a fear of dirt
Scoleciphobia	a fear of worms
Seplophobia	a fear of decaying matter
Spheksophobia	a fear of wasps

90 *Number of African farmers who rely on seed saving for
planting their food crops the following year*

FLOWERY PHRASES

To take the primrose path
To take a path of self-indulgence that ends in ruin.

To lay something up in lavender
To treat something as very precious.

To nip something in the bud
To prevent a plan before it's acted on.

To talk of an old chestnut
To talk of a hackneyed phrase or an over-used old joke.

To make hay from someone
To make money out of someone else's mistakes.

To seize the nettle
To take severe action to overcome a difficult situation.

To be lily-livered
To be cowardly.

To be a shrinking violet
To be a timid person who shies away from attention.

To be a lotus-eater
To neglect your friends and family to enjoy a life of luxury.

To be a thorn in the flesh
To be a source of constant annoyance.

To sit on thorns
To be in an embarrassing or difficult situation.

To eat the seed corn
To spend capital and destroy the source of income.

LOVE IN THE GARDEN

Henry II created a garden for his wife, Eleanor of Aquitaine, at Winchester and a romantic bower for his mistress, Rosamund Clifford, at Woodstock. The bower was a grand affair with three cottages and a water garden fed by a spring. Word of the bower quickly spread, starting a trend for Rosamund bowers throughout the country. But the popularity of Henry and Rosamund's love garden may well have been poor Rosamund's undoing – rumour has it that when word of the garden reached Eleanor's ear, she had Henry's mistress murdered. When hearing of her death, the poor King Henry II was apparently so full of despair that he ordered she be disinterred so that he could say a final goodbye. But as the inscription on her tomb would seem to indicate, he wasn't that happy with what he discovered:

Hic jacet in tumba Rosa Mundi, non Rosa Munda
Non redolet, sed olet, quae redolere solet

Here Rose the grace, not Rose the chaste, reposes.
The scent that rises is not the scent of roses

ON THE GRAPEVINE

What a summer, what a summer!
This is magic indeed.
And how, I ask you, did it come to us
Unsought and undeserved?

Very often, last summer, I felt just like that. What happiness it is to work from dawn to dusk for your family and yourself, to build a roof over their head, to till the soil to feed them, to create your own world, like Robinson Crusoe, in imitation of the Creator of the universe and to bring forth your life, as if you were your own mother, again and again.

So many new thoughts come into your head when your hands are busy with hard physical work, when your mind has set you a task which can be achieved by physical effort and which brings its reward in joy and success, when for six hours on end you dig or hammer, scorched by the life-giving breath of the sky. And it isn't a loss but a gain that these transient thoughts, intuitions, analogies, are not put down on paper but forgotten.

Boris Pasternak, *Doctor Zhivago*

THE DEEP FREEZE

Evidence suggests that two million years ago, there were hundreds of species of plants in Britain, but the Ice Age was to change everything. With most of Britain covered with ice more than 2,000ft deep, many plants (and animals) retreated south to escape the big freeze. When the Ice Age ended, about 10,000 years ago, plants that had moved southward gradually began to return and re-colonise Britain, but the melt water that created the English Channel about 6,000 years ago, cut Britain off from both mainland Europe and many of the returning species. Ivy, marjoram, water mint and holly are just some of the survivors who managed to make it back in time.

How is it possible to tell what was around during the Ice Age and what wasn't? It's simple really. Scientists are able to examine preserved strands of pollen found by boring deep down through the earth to layers of plant matter that go back hundreds and thousands of years.

QUOTE UNQUOTE

It is a blessed sort of work, and if Eve had had a spade in Paradise and known what to do with it, we should not have had all that sad business of the apple.
ELIZABETH VON ARNIM, countess and novelist

There has been much speculation over the years about the origin of the Cox's Orange Pippin, England's most famous apple, which has managed to come to considerable fame without anybody knowing much about where it came from.

According to the fifth edition of *Hogg's Fruit Manual*, published in 1884, Cox's Orange Pippin originated in 1830 from a pip of Ribston pippin and was 'raised at Colnbrook Lawn, near Slough, Bucks, by a Mr Cox who was formerly a brewer at Bermondsey'. This entry was, however, contested by another entry in the same book, which claimed that the much-loved apple was in fact raised by Squire Cox at Cranford.

In 1934, a third account published in *The Times* shed more light on the mystery. According to the anonymous author, Mr Cox was actually Richard Cox who was born in the 1770s and had indeed been a brewer at Bermondsey who had retired to Colnbrook. This claim appeared to be backed up by the 1841 census, which listed Richard Cox as a resident at Lawn Cottage in Colnbrook with his wife, two maidservants, a boy for domestic work and three labourers. *The Times'* article provided further details, including the information that the original Cox's Orange Pippin tree had grown in the vegetable garden at Lawn Cottage,

but was believed to have been blown down in about 1911.

But while *The Times* provided conclusive details about the owner, the crucial question of how the tree came about was still unclear. Frustratingly, there are several different accounts. According to one, which was published in *The Garden* in 1876, two pips of the Ribston variety were sown in a pot, one of which turned out to be a Cox's Orange Pippin and the other a Cox's Pomona. A second version, published in *The Gardener's Magazine* in 1902, states that nine pips were sown, one of which turned out to be an Orange Pippin, and the other the Pomona. According to the latter, the Ribston fruit from which the pips were taken from had been pollinated by a Blenheim Orange. A third unpublished and less likely version is that Mrs Cox watched a bee fertilizing a blossom, tied a piece of ribbon on the branch as a mark and then cultivated the pips.

And when did the eureka Orange Pippin moment happen? Again, we have no idea, but it must have been prior to 1857, since the first commercial mention of a Cox's Orange Pippin was in *The Gardener's Chronicle* in 1857. Following its ignominious debut, the apple swiftly became a popular dessert apple, earning second place in the 1883 National Apple Congress at Chiswick.

ON THE GRAPEVINE

Hari and I got into the habit of going to the bibighar, and sitting there in the pavilion, because it was the one place in Mayapore where we could be together and be utterly natural with each other. And even then there was the feeling that we were having to hide ourselves away from the inquisitive, the amused, and the disapproving. Going in there, through the archway, or standing up and getting ready to go back into the cantonment – those were the moments when this feeling of being about to hide or about to come out of hiding to face things was strongest. And even while we were there, there was often a feeling of preparedness, in case someone came in and saw us together, even though we were doing nothing but sitting side by side on the edge of the mosaic 'platform' with our feet dangling, like two kids sitting on a wall. But at least we could be pretty sure no white man or woman would come into the gardens. They never did. The gardens always seemed to have a purely Indian connection, just as the maidan really had a purely English one.

Paul Scott, *The Jewel in the Crown*

ANNUAL INTOXICATION

The delicate flowers of the *Lonicera* (honeysuckle) bush are one of the most intoxicating fragrances in the garden. Most gardeners grow summer varieties, but when plants are carefully chosen, honeysuckle can flower nearly all year round.

Honeysuckle variety	Flowering period
Lonicera fragrantissima	December to February
Lonicera x purpusii	December to February
Lonicera americana	April to June
Lonicera nitida	May
Lonicera periclymenum 'Belgica'	May to June
Lonicera japonica 'Halliana'	July to September
Lonicera periclymenum 'Serotina'	July to October

THE WORLD'S SMALLEST

The world's smallest flowering plant, the *Wolffia globosa*, is a member of the duckweed family. With no leaves, stems or roots, this minute flowering beauty consists of spheres less than 1mm long which cover the surface of water. *Wolffia* are usually transported from pond to pond on the feet of waterfowl, but they have also been found in the water of melted hailstones and are reputed to have been carried in tornadoes. The *Wolffia globulosa* is on average 0.6mm long and 0.3mm wide and weighs the equivalent of two grains of table salt. In fact a bouquet of 12 *Wolffia globulosa* flowers would fit easily on a pinhead!

94 *Percentage of peatbogs that have been damaged or destroyed in the UK – mainly to provide compost for gardeners*

HOW DOES A MUSHROOM GROW?

A single mushroom can produce millions of spores which are dispersed in a variety of ways. Once they reach the ground they germinate and form mycelium. The mycelium is made of many microscopic filaments called 'hyphae' which form a branching thread that spreads like a web for several metres in order to absorb nutrients. If conditions are right a mushroom will grow.

BLOOMING PUZZLES

I have two arms, but no fingers or hands. I have two feet, but cannot run. I carry best with my feet OFF the ground.
What am I?
Answer on page 153

WARTIME ADVICE

Weight, in pounds, to which a Cycad lepidozamia cone can grow 95

KISSING UNDER THE MISTLETOE

The custom of kissing to seal a betrothal dates back to the Roman period, a ritual that – along with steam baths and St Valentine's day – filtered through Europe. It is not clear, however, from where the tradition of kissing under the mistletoe originates but here are a few theories:

An old English aphrodisiac
The Celts believed mistletoe was a sacred plant that brought luck and sexuality to couples, and it was widely used it in marriage rites.

A Scandinavian symbol of forgiveness
According to Scandinavian mythology, an arrow of mistletoe was used to kill the god of sunshine and light by Loki, the god of mischief. The plant was forgiven for its murderous role and reborn in Scandinavian hearts as a symbol of love to be kissed under.

Lurve… the Babylonian way
In Babylon, in the 9th century BC, single women would shower praise on the goddess of beauty and love by standing beneath the mistletoe that adorned her temple. Following this ritual each devotee was expected to bond with the first man who approached her.

Over time, the two traditions, the sacredness of mistletoe and the practice of celebrating a betrothal with a kiss, combined and it was soon believed that couples who kissed under the mistletoe to seal their engagement were assured fertility, good fortune and a long and happy married life. And it is from these hopeful origins that the custom of tipsily kissing under the mistletoe at Christmas time emerges.

SIX GARDEN PROVERBS

A book is like a garden carried in the pocket.
The earth laughs at him who calls a place his own.
Better eat vegetables and fear no creditors, than eat duck
and hide from them.
Fine words butter no parsnips.
The rose has thorns only for those who would gather it.
Tickle it with a hoe and it will laugh into a harvest.

GARDENS OF HISTORY

Charles I was sitting in Chelsea Palace garden when the renowned Italian sculptor Gian Lorenzo Bernini's bust of the king was delivered. The hapless Charles ordered the bust to be brought into the garden and uncovered, whereupon a hawk with a bird in his beak flew overhead, and a drop of blood fell on its throat.

NUDE BUT NOT LEWD

According to a 2001 national opinion poll, 66% of respondents believed nudity in the back garden was OK and 10% believed that nudity in some areas of public parks was acceptable.

LONDON'S SECRET GARDENS

The Chelsea Physic Garden was established in Chelsea in 1673 by the Society of Apothecaries, at a time when doctors relied almost exclusively on administering plants to patients for treatment. Situated by the River Thames to allow its non-native species to benefit from a warmer micro-climate, it was not only a training centre for physicians and apothecaries, but also a treatment centre where the poor could line up to be cured.

The gardens might not have survived until today, had it not been for Sir Hans Sloane, an Irish physician and keen botanist. He made a fortune as a physician to the rich and famous (and also the poor and destitute, providing they turned up at his practice before 10am) and with his wealth, bought the country area around the Chelsea Physic Garden in 1713. Sir Hans bequeathed the Chelsea Physic Garden to the Society of Apothecaries for the permanent price of £5 per year; a sum that is still paid to his descendants today.

The Chelsea Physic Garden remains committed to its historical role in promoting the study of botany in relation to medicine and healing arts. It remains closely linked to the London College of Physicians and continues to be a major contributor to the study and preservation of plant species. It holds over 7,000 different species, and contains a pharmaceutical garden where beds are arranged according to drug use; a world medicine section that demonstrates the use of plants in treatment by different peoples all over the world; an aromatherapy section; and a seed collection library in association with the Henry Doubleday Research Association.

FANTASY GARDENS

Years ago, Swiss sculptor Niki de Saint-Phalle dreamt of an enchanted garden populated by vast glittering creatures who smiled on her benevolently. In 1978, the artist finally realised her dream when she started constructing The Tarot Garden on the side of a hill in southern Tuscany. With huge sculptures of bright mosaics, based on Tarot card figures, this truly extraordinary vision remains unfinished, despite many years of work. Saint-Phalle remains dedicated to her dream, appropriately living inside the sculpture of an enormous empress.

DIVIDE AND PULL

Some perennials like to be divided every year, while others object to being divided at all. The best time to divide is in the autumn, after a good watering.

Divide annually
Big-root geraniums • Obedient plant
Spiderwort • Yarrow

Divide every two to three years
Aster • Bee balm
Evening primrose • Painted daisy
Sneezewood

Divide when needed
Artemisia • Astilbe
Bellflower • Cranesbill
Dahlia • Daylily
False rockcress • Hosta
Lamb's ears • Larkspur
Lily-of-the-valley • Pampas grass
Pincushion flower • Pink
Purple coneflower • Snow-in-summer
Speedwell • Stonecrop
Sweet woodruff • Tickseed

Not to be divided
Bleeding heart • Carolina lupine
Hellebore • Cinnamon fern
Columbine • False indigo
Foxtail Lily • Gas plant
Lupine • Oriental poppy

FANTASY GARDENS

Early in the morning on a bowling green in Buckinghamshire, a groundsman named Chris Parsons gets up before dawn to drag a large rag brush across the dew-soaked grass. The result, at the Dew Gardens in Aylesbury, is a pattern of extraordinary beauty – somewhat reminiscent of a Bridget Riley op-art – that lasts so briefly. As the sun comes up to light the dew, it glitters in a few seconds of momentary glory and then vanishes as if it never existed. Fortunately Chris Parsons, who made his dew-art discovery by accident, has made a more permanent record, using a camera set up on a tree in the corner.

QUOTE UNQUOTE

After his majesty has eaten the cabbage I fancy he wants to have the whole garden also.
JOHN DUDLEY,
Tudor politician on hearing of the King of France's ambitions to conquer England

DUSK IN THE GARDEN

Carnation, Lily, Lily, Rose is one of John Singer Sargent's most famous works of art. This pre-Raphaelite painting depicts a mythic idyll of two little girls lighting enormous Japanese lanterns in the dusk of a beautiful garden.

But the autumnal garden twilight Sargent wished to capture was so fleeting, he could only paint during the dusky evenings of autumn and the painting took over a year to complete. Indeed, so brief was the available and right light, that the girls who modelled for this timeless masterpiece, had to be carefully posed with their lanterns in the garden just before sunset each evening and wait for the right light to appear.

And as winter approached, the flowers in the garden began to die off, forcing Sargent to replace them with cut stocks that were carefully hidden in pots, so that he could keep on painting.

ON THE GRAPEVINE

Ophelia: There's fennel for you, and columbines: there's rue for you; and here's some for me: we may call it herb-grace o' Sundays: O you must wear your rue with a difference. There's a daisy: I would give you some violets, but they withered all when my father died: they say he made a good end, [Sings] For bonny sweet Robin is all my joy.
William Shakespeare, *Hamlet, Act IV, Scene 5*

WHAT'S IN A NAME?

To differentiate flowers from each other, the Chinese devised elaborate – and charming – names for each of them, such as 'Sunlight in the forest', 'Water that slumbers beneath the moon', and 'My frock is no longer pure white because in tearing it the son of heaven left a small ruby stain'.

BLOOMING PUZZLES

A snail sees a row of fresh lettuces at the top
of a sloped garden, 20m away.
Every day he climbs 5m up the slope, but at night slides 4m back.
How many days will it take him to reach the lettuces?
Answer on Page 153

THE HEIGHT OF A GARDEN HEDGE

The law requires house sellers to declare any formal disputes they have had with neighbours to potential buyers. Not declaring the war you've been waging with your neighbour for the last 10 years could land you in legal hot water.

One of the commonest disputes between neighbours is over the height of garden hedges. There are an estimated 100,000 hedge disputes going on all over Britain. And because until recently there was no satisfactory recourse to law, gardeners who had their light blocked by a neighbour's high hedge could do nothing about it. Now, under the *Anti-social Behaviour Act* of 2003, local authorities can issue notices requiring hedges to be cut down, although they cannot be removed altogether. People tend to develop a fortress mentality over their own properties. Arguments can often get out of hand and will too frequently end up in the courts... or worse. At least two people have been murdered as a result of hedge disputes.

If your hedge is high, think about the effect it has on your neighbour's property – does it cut out their sunlight? And if you are having a problem with a neighbour's hedge and can't seem to solve it amicably, contact Hedgeline – a support group for victims of high hedge disputes.

GARDENERS IN FICTION

Samwise Gamgee is the loyal servant of Frodo in the *Lord of the Rings* trilogy. A fellow hobbit, Sam happily lived an uneventful life in the shire as the gardener of Bag End. When Gandalf told Frodo about the Ring, Sam was selected to be Frodo's companion on the journey to Rivendell. He was also part of the fellowship of the Ring. Sam was portrayed by Sean Astin in the Peter Jackson trilogy. Astin had to gain two stone for his part as hobbits are considered to be somewhat portly.

CUCKOO'S PINTLE

Instructions for use: Place one pintle in the sole of your shoe.
Note: Pulling power cannot be guaranteed (see page 71).

see page 71

NEIGHBOURS FROM HELL

Some plants are lifelong enemies! Keep them away from each other, or it will end in tears:

Plant	Enemy	Reason
Bean	Onion	Onion will stunt bean's growth
Carrot	Dill	Dill will stunt carrot's growth
Cucumber	Sage	Sage will stunt cucumber's growth
Pea	Onion	Onion will stunt pea's growth
Potato	Tomato	They are both attacked by the same blights
Pumpkin	Potato	Potato will inhibit pumpkin's growth
Tomato	Sweetcorn	Attracts worms that feed on tomatoes
Turnip	Potato	Potato will inhibit turnip's growth

THE LOST GARDENS OF HELIGAN

The Lost Gardens of Heligan, situated near St Austell in Cornwall, were occupied by the Tremayne family from the 16th century to World War I. During the 19th century, the family created the extraordinarily beautiful garden, which comprised: 58 acres of plantings; almost 100 acres of ornamental woodlands; and flowers, trees and shrubs that had been carefully collected from all over the globe.

During World War I, the male gardeners all signed with the Duke of Cornwall's light infantry and Heligan House was taken over by the War Office. Only six of the 22 gardeners returned from the battles in Flanders, and increasing costs eventually forced the Tremaynes to rent the house out. The family who took over were not able to keep up the garden.

In World War II, the US army took over to practice their D-Day landings on a nearby beach. Still the garden remained untouched and in 1970 the Tremaynes divided the house up into flats and sold them off. By this time the gardens, still owned by the Tremaynes, lay forgotten.

But in February 1990 a chance meeting between John Willis, a descendant of the Tremaynes, and the current owners of the grounds Tim Smit and John Nelson, changed everything for Heligan's beautiful overgrown gardens. A 10-year restoration project uncovered and brought back to full beauty some of the most extraordinary treasures of the gardening world.

These include: two and a half miles of footpaths that were discovered under 10ft high brambles; Flora's Green, a lawn used by ladies for dancing which is surrounded by rhododendrons that are more than 150 years old; a sundial garden described in 1896 as having the finest herbaceous border in England; and one of the best beehole walls in the country, with 15 vaulted hive chambers to encourage bees to pollinate the plants.

The gardens also include some of the world's largest trees, including the largest Japanese black pine, Chinese cedar and Chilean yew. Reopened to the public in 1998, over 200,000 visitors have seen the Lost Gardens of Heligan restored to their former glory.

A BARBARIC FRUIT

Rhubarb owes its name to the geopolitics of the Roman Empire. The Romans called it 'Rha' after the river along which they first discovered it (now known as the River Volga in western Russia) and 'barbarum' because the territory it grew in was not part of the Roman empire.

GIRLS' FLOWERY NAMES

Aside from the Cherrys, Jasmines, Hollys and other well-known flowery names given to girls, there are some whose meanings are a little less obvious:

Anthea ....like a flower
Antonia .... flowering and flourishing
Aurora ....dawn
Bronwen..white blossomed
Carmen...garden paradise
Chloe ....flourishing green shoot
Daphne ....laurel (after the Greek goddess of music fled from
                                        Apollo he transformed her into a laurel bush)
Hazel ....fruit of wisdom
Rosalie ....feast of roses (rosalia is the annual Roman ceremony
                                        of hanging rose-garland on tombs)

PLANTING BY POSTCODE

In an attempt to improve biodiversity by encouraging gardeners to grow native species, the Natural History Museum has set up a post-code plant database. By entering your postcode you can find out which plants are native to your garden. Trees native to the postcode E8 (Hackney, London) are:

Alder	*Alnus glutinosa*
Ash	*Fraxinus excelsior*
Aspen	*Populus tremula*
Crack-willow	*Salix fragilis*
English elm	*Ulmus procera*
Hornbeam	*Carpinus betulus*
Pedunculate oak	*Quercus robur*
Silver birch	*Betula pendula*
White willow	*Salix alba*
Wild cherry	*Prunus avium*
Wych elm	*Ulmus glabra*

DRIFTING TO ENGLAND

Few pleasures can match finding an exotic seed on a grey English beach. Seeds which have been found include the Caribbean nickernut and the enormous seeds of the tropical vine *Entada gigas* on Scotland's western coast. The curious crucifix-like markings of *Merremia discoidesperma* led discoverers on the Outer Hebrides to name it Mary's seed and regard it with considerable reverence.

However, there was the hill full in sight, so there was nothing to be done but start again. This time she came upon a large flower-bed, with a border of daisies, and a willow-tree growing in the middle.

'O Tiger-lily!' said Alice, addressing herself to one that was waving gracefully about in the wind, 'I wish you could talk!'

'We can talk!' said the Tiger-lily, 'when there's anybody worth talking to.' Alice was so astonished that she couldn't speak for a minute: it quite seemed to take her breath away. At length, as the Tiger-lily only went on waving about, she spoke again, in a timid voice – almost in a whisper. 'And can all the flowers talk?'

'As well as you can,' said the Tiger-lily. 'And a great deal louder.'

'It isn't manners for us to begin, you know,' said the Rose, 'and I really was wondering when you'd speak! Said I to myself, "Her face has got some sense in it, though it's not a clever one!" Still, you're the right colour, and that goes a long way.' 'I don't care about the colour,' the Tiger-lily remarked. 'If only her petals curled up a little more, she'd be all right.'

Alice didn't like being criticised, so she began asking questions. 'Aren't you sometimes frightened at being planted out here, with nobody to take care

of you?' 'There's the tree in the middle,' said the Rose. 'What else is it good for?'

'But what could it do, if any danger came?' Alice asked.

'It could bark,' said the Rose.

'It says "Boughwough!"' cried a Daisy. 'That's why its branches are called boughs!'

'Didn't you know that?' cried another Daisy. And here they all began shouting together, till the air seemed quite full of little shrill voices. 'Silence, every one of you!' cried the Tiger-lily, waving itself passionately from side to side, and trembling with excitement. 'They know I can't get at them!' it panted, bending its quivering head towards Alice, 'or they wouldn't dare to do it!'

'Never mind!' Alice said in a soothing tone, and, stooping down to the daisies, who were just beginning again, she whispered 'If you don't hold your tongues, I'll pick you!'

There was silence in a moment, and several of the pink daisies turned white.

'That's right!' said the Tiger-lily. 'The daisies are worst of all. When one speaks, they all begin together, and it's enough to make one wither to hear the way they go on!'

'How is it you can all talk so nicely?' Alice said, hoping to get it into a better temper by a compliment. 'I've been in many gardens before, but none of the flowers could talk.'

Lewis Carroll, *Alice Through the Looking Glass*

QUOTE UNQUOTE

Gardening is the slowest of performing arts.
ANONYMOUS

KEY TO THE MAZE?

One of the most famous hedge mazes in the world is situated at Hampton Court near London. It covers an area of a third of an acre (about 1,350 square metres), and its paths are half a mile long. Planted in the Hampton Court Palace Gardens in 1702, it still attracts people from all over the world, and every year thousands of them are happy 'to be lost' in it.

To solve you must apparently turn L, R, R, L, L, L, but the Jerome K Jerome extract on page 62 should help to confuse matters further.

CELEBRITIES IN THE GARDEN

Ever since the invention of long lenses, the paparazzi have secretly snapped celebrities in the privacy of their own gardens. Whether sun-bathing topless, like Amanda Holden, or bottomless, like Sara Cox on her honeymoon, or in the act of toe-sucking her financial advisor, like Sarah Ferguson, these pictures have been splashed across the tabloid pages for all the world to see. But with new tougher laws on their side, celebrities are fighting back – and earning a nice little settlement in compensation:

Julie Goodyear
Lynched by a photographer with a long lens in her garden
No compensation sought

Sarah Cox
Photographed nude in a garden on a private island
Won £50,000 from The People

Robbie Williams and Rachel Hunter
Steamy photos of the pair indulging in some alfresco nookie
No complaint was made – leading some to suspect the pictures were fakes

Catherine Zeta Jones
Reportedly shot topless, pregnant and smoking on the internet
Picture withdrawn after threat of legal action

Amanda Holden
Photographed topless in a garden in Italy
Won £40,000 compensation from The People

Jennifer Aniston
Snapped topless in her garden
Agreed a US$550,000 settlement with publishers

13 GARLICKY FACTS

Thought to be one of the oldest cultivated food plants in the world, garlic has been used in cooking and for medicinal purposes for more than 6,000 years.

• The name garlic is believed to be of Anglo-Saxon origin, derived from *gar* (a spear) and *lac* (a plant), in reference to the shape of its leaves.

• Garlic is a member of the lily family, and its origin is unknown, although it is believed to have spread from central Asia through the Mediterranean.

• According to legend, when Satan left the garden of Eden, a garlic plant sprang from the grass where he placed his left foot.

• Homer's epic hero Ulysses was saved from being transformed into a pig by garlic.

• Egyptian kings gave garlic to the workmen building the pyramids in the belief that it increased their stamina.

• In Imperial Rome, garlic was used to repel scorpions and treat dog bites, leprosy and asthma.

• A long-standing remedy for worms involves hanging garlic around the neck. It was believed that the smell would suffocate the worms (if not the wearer).

• In some parts of Europe, runners still believe that they have more chance of winning a race if they chew a piece of garlic.

• Hungarian jockeys will apparently fasten a clove of garlic to their saddle before a race, believing the other horses will fall back to avoid the smell.

• According to Cole's *Art of Simpling*, if you plant garlic in a garden infested with moles, it will force them to 'leap out of the ground presently'.

• In 1858, Louis Pasteur discovered garlic was capable of killing bacteria. During World War I, it was used to dress wounds and treat gangrene. It is also useful for athlete's foot, replacing, as it were, one strong smell for another.

• Garlic is also believed to have a positive effect in lowering blood pressure and cholesterol, reducing the possibility of strokes, thrombosis and yeast infections. It may also help protect the body from cancer.

• While its vampire protection potential may not as yet be fully tested, garlic is a natural insect repellent, and some farmers are even spraying their fields with it. In the garden, garlic oil has an adverse effect on slugs and snails, causing them to 'dry up'. It is also an effective deterrent against fleas when rubbed into the fur of domestic animals.

Amount, in milligrams, of potassium contained in a boiled, drained, edible pumpkin flower

COMMON DIGGING MISTAKES TO AVOID

1. Digging in bare feet or flip flops.
2. Jumping on the spade a mite too enthusiastically with both feet.
3. Not bending your knees.
4. Flicking the soil ineffectually into your face.
5. Putting all the strain of the work on your back.

ON THE GRAPEVINE

How various his employment, whom the world
Calls idle; and who justly in return
Esteems that busy world an idler too!
Friends, books, a garden and perhaps his pen,
Delightful industry enjoyed at home
And nature in her cultivated trim,
Dressed to his taste, inviting him abroad –
Can he want occupation who has these?

William Cowper, *The Task*

THE LOST GARDENS OF LAVENDER ROAD

In July 2003, residents of Lavender Road in East London were evacuated after their gardens began to disappear into an enormous hole, which had suddenly appeared during digging for the Channel Tunnel link: 'We looked down and sure enough, it had gone, two gardens had gone, all I could see was a hole', said resident Harry Kearsley. But the Lavender Road residents are not the only British residents to have lost their gardens. Indeed losing a garden underground appears to happen a little too often to be comfortable:

In January 2002, two homes in West Cornwall faced demolition after an old tin mine shaft opened up in their gardens in St Ives. Robert Spenser, who had lived in his house for 23 years, was reportedly devastated.

In February 2002, an astonishing 200ft mine shaft opened up in a garden in Redruth, Cornwall. The owners of the house were alerted to the hole's appearance after a surprised neighbour heard a 'thunderous sound' when he went to collect his car. The hole is apparently part of a network of mining tunnels which date back to medieval times but have not been used since 1890.

In December 2003, a 20ft mine shaft opened up in a garden in Moxley, near Darlington and a dog, which had fallen in it, had to be rescued. Four years previously, a house in the same street had to be destroyed after it fell down the same collapsed mine shaft.

BLOOMING PUZZLES

What is the difference between a mycologist, a mycophile
and a mycophagist?
Answer on page 153

RETURN OF THE NATIVE

Native tree species support a far higher population of insect species
than exotic immigrants. Tropical trees might look pretty, have big
flowers or fancy leaf-shapes, but let's face it, when it comes to providing
life for insects, birds and mammals, they're practically barren. But take
our treasured oak down under and it would be the same; it might be
greeted enthusiastically by gardeners, but most insects would turn their
noses up in disgust.

Tree Species	Number of insect species it supports
Oak (*Quercus*)	284
Willow (*Salix*)	266
Birch (*Betula*)	229
Hawthorn (*Crataegus*)	149
Blackthorn (*Prunus*)	109
Pine (*Pinus*)	91
Alder (*Alnus*)	90
Elm (*Ulmus*)	82
Beech (*Fagus*)	64
Ash (*Fraxinus*)	41
Lime (*Tilia*)	31
Hornbeam (*Carpinus*)	28

CELEBRITY GARDENERS

Diarmuid Gavin is famed as a maverick garden designer with an
unpronounceable name and an Irish accent so broad that comedian
Graham Norton described it a speech impediment. Diarmuid's
innovative designs, complete with metals, mosaics and sardine cans,
are sometimes so weird and outrageous that viewers simply tune in to
Home Front in the Garden just to see what he comes up with next.
Diarmuid is equally famed for his no-nonsense approach to clothing –
particularly the white teeshirt with 69 emblazoned across the front
that he claims he doesn't wear on every show. It was a joy then, to see
him paired up with the obsessively over-dressed Laurence Llewelyn-
Bowen (and hear Diarmuid ask: 'What are you wearin' the wife's
curtains for?'). Contrary to his television designs, Diarmuid's own
garden is surprisingly normal – with an elegant rectangular lawn.

A FEELING FOR FOLIAGE

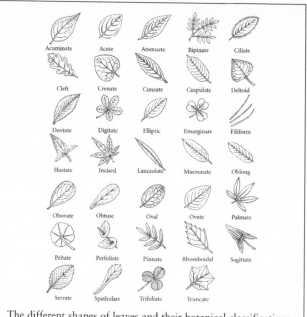

Acuminate · Acute · Attenuate · Bipinnate · Ciliate

Cleft · Crenate · Cuneate · Cuspidate · Deltoid

Dentate · Digitate · Elliptic · Emarginate · Filiform

Hastate · Incised · Lanceolate · Mucronate · Oblong

Obovate · Obtuse · Oval · Ovate · Palmate

Peltate · Perfoliate · Pinnate · Rhomboidal · Sagittate

Serrate · Spathulate · Trifoliate · Truncate

The different shapes of leaves and their botanical classifications.

NINE PLANTS THAT THINK THEY'RE ANIMALS

Clianthus puniceus	Parrot's bill
Ilex ferox	Hedgehog holly
Hedera helix	Dragon's claw ivy
Acanthus mollis	Bear's breeches
Stachys byzantina	Lamb's ears/Bunnies' ears
Chenopodium album	Lamb's quarters/Fat hen
Acalypha hispida	Monkey tail
Heliconia rostrata	Lobster claws
Silene pendula	Nodding catchfly

HOMEGROWN TALENT

Ever wondered where your favourite plants come from? A closer look at their Latin names might help:

Name	From
Alchemilla	Arabic
Amelanchier	French
Aucuba	Japanese
Babania	Dutch
Berberis	Arabic
Camassia	North American Indian
Cichorium	Egyptian
Genista	Celtic
Gingko	Chinese
Hoheria	Maori
Hyssopus	Hebrew
Jasminium	Persian
Trollius	German
Tulipa	Turkish
Yucca	Caribbean

THE SYCAMORE TREE MARTYRS

On the village green in Tolpuddle in Dorset stands a vast, ancient Sycamore Tree. It was under this tree in 1834 that George Loveless and five other labourers gathered after their agricultural labourer's wage was cut from seven to six shillings a week – a piffling amount for families on an average weekly wage of 13s 9d. The six formed a union to negotiate higher wages but were promptly arrested and tried under the Mutinies Act for apparently swearing an illegal oath. Found guilty, the six were deported to Australia, where they might well have remained, had it not been for the support of more than 200,000 fellow workers who rallied in London and signed a petition demanding the return of the Tolpuddle Martyrs. The men were subsequently returned, and the tree underneath whose branches it all started still stands today.

QUOTE UNQUOTE

Oak before Ash, we'll be in for a splash
Ash before Oak, we'll be in for a soak.

A traditional rain warning determined by which tree's leaves – oak or ash – are unfurled first in spring.

FAMOUS GARDNERS

Ava Gardner
American movie actress who starred in 66 movies and married three times, to Micky Rooney, Artie Shaw and Frank Sinatra.

Rulon Gardner
A Greco-Roman wrestling champion who began wrestling when six years old and became Olympic Champion at the Sydney Olympics in 2000.

Gerald Gardner
Known as the 'father of modern witchcraft', Gerald published a book called *Witchcraft Today* and formed one of the first covens in modern English history in 1939 near the New Forest.

Erle Stanley Gardner
The creator of Perry Mason, Erle wrote a total of 82 novels about one of America's favourite detectives.

Archibald Gardner
Founder of Gardner Village in Utah, Archibald believed in the doctrine of plural marriage, had 11 wives, 48 children and 270 grandchildren. Go Archibald!

John Gardner
Novelist who successfully took over from Ian Fleming to become the official writer of James Bond novels, including *License Renewed* (1981), *Icebreaker* (1983), *Nobody Lives Forever* (1986), *No Deals, Mr Bond* (1987) and *Win, Lose or Die* (1989).

Janine Gardner
Winner of Utah's 'Funniest Person Award' in 1996, Janine does comedy routines for US lingerie giant, Victoria's Secret.

Dale A Gardner
American astronaut who has spent 337 hours in space and orbited the world's gardens 225 times.

Isabella Stewart Gardner
Traveller, art collector and aficionado of horse-racing also known as Mrs Jack, this fast lady's mottos were 'win as though you are used to it and lose as if you like it' and 'don't spoil a good story by telling the truth'. Predictably Isabella scandalised the polite American society she lived in, but left a legacy of some of the world's finest paintings, including the works by Botticelli, Vermeer and Rembrandt on display in the Isabella Stewart Gardner museum in Boston.

GARDEN ETIQUETTE

The word etiquette is derived from the old French word *estiquette*, or label. *Estiquettes* were first used by a gardener who worked at the fabulous Royal Gardens at Versailles. He put up signs to keep disrespectful members of the court off Louis XIV's treasured grass lawns. The signs were rudely ignored by all, until in desperation the king firmly decreed that no one was to walk beyond the *estiquette*.

QUOTE UNQUOTE

*Science, or para-science, tells us that geraniums bloom better if they
are spoken to. But a kind word every now and then is really quite
enough. Too much attention, like too much feeding, and weeding
and hoeing, inhibits and embarrasses them.*
VICTORIA GLENDINNING, novelist

GARDENERS IN FICTION

After Jerzy Kosinski published *Being There* in 1971, he received a
telegram purporting to be from the novel's main character 'Chance
the Gardener'. When Kosinski rang the number, Peter Sellers
answered, and what followed is often considered to be the actor's best
work; the satire of a simple-minded gardener who reveals through his
innocence the self-deceiving nature of society.

THE MYSTERY OF THE
CATTLEYA LABIATA VERA

In 1818, plant collector William
Cattley discovered some curious
sections of an unknown plant in a
box of lichens sent to him from
Brazil. Intrigued, he managed to
get the plant to flower into a
beautiful orchid with a
pronounced lip, and it was
promptly named in his honour
(*Cattleya labiata vera*).

Because of its astonishing
beauty and ability to flower in
England, its reputation swiftly
spread and before long, it had
reached the top position on the
wish lists of plant hunters as far as
South America. Yet frustratingly,
it could not be found. As the
remaining divisions of Cattley's
specimens gradually died off,
other pieces would from time to
time tantalisingly turn up in
auction rooms. In 1880, a rare
specimen was sold for 39 guineas,
the equivalent of £1,800 today.

But while *Cattleya labiata vera*
remained elusive, other orchid
specimens were causing quite a
stir in horticultural circles. This
was in part due to the Duke of
Devonshire, who had, with the
help of his celebrated gardener
Joseph Paxton, found a way in
which they could thrive and
flower. As the prices of rare
orchids soared, competition
between orchid hunters
intensified, each attempting to
prevent competitors from finding
rare orchids, particularly the
'lost' *Cattleya labiata vera*.

It wasn't until the 1890s that
Cattleya labiata vera was finally
located, and when it was, it was
found growing in such
abundance that overnight, it
went from being a rare to a
commonplace variety. Today, it is
the most well-known of all
orchid plants.

HAUNTED GARDENS

The Botanic Gardens in Ventnor, on the Isle of Wight, are built on the site of a former Royal National Hospital for Chest Diseases, and patients who suffered a lingering and debilitating death from tuberculosis are still believed to haunt the site.

When workmen started to demolish the hospital to build the garden in 1969, they experienced many unexplained and spine-chilling events. Firstly, all their machinery failed (they were forced to tackle the operating theatre with sledgehammers), and then they claimed to be haunted by the ghost of a consumptive young girl watching them as they worked. Subsequent visitors also claimed to hear sounds of weeping and moaning, and a ghostly nurse has been sighted doing her rounds in the gardens. As for the slight hint of cinnamon, which pervades the site of the old outside wards (now the potting sheds), this has been linked to the patients' Christmas pick-me-up cinnamon punch. If you're lucky (or unlucky – whichever way you look at it), you may be one of the few who see the whole hospital building itself appear, arising like a shattered mist out of the ghostly beauty of the garden.

THE CURSE OF THE BLACK HELLEBORE

Black hellebore leaves were reputedly used by witches for charms and spells. So evil were its leaves, that even collecting this plant was considered a dangerous task. According to the natural historian, Pliny the Elder, gatherers had to draw a circle round the plant with a sword and seek permission from the gods to lift the plant from the ground. Gatherers were also advised to look east and avoid being witnessed by an eagle for if they were, they might die within a year.

ON THE GRAPEVINE

I like to wear my gloves while gardening
They surely stop my hands from hardening
But has it occurred to you
That a pack with two is one too few?
For while my right is thin and worn
My left is new and scarcely worn.
So what about a spare left or right
To overcome this gardener's plight?
Or failing this I hope to find
A South Paw with the same in mind

Shirley Ernest, *Plea*

Number of tea gardens in Darjeeling growing tea in 1874 113

The 1928 DH Lawrence novel *Lady Chatterley's Lover*, centres around the love affair between Lady Chatterley – whose wheelchair-bound husband has been rendered impotent by his war wounds – and a gamekeeper/gardener at their estate. The book contained passages of sex and four letter words – in one memorable extract, Lady Chatterley and her lover frolicked together in the garden naked.

Anticipating reactions to his book, Lawrence decided to publish 1,000 copies of *Lady Chatterley's Lover* privately in Florence in 1928. The copies were secretly distributed by his friends and by the end of the year, had sold out. Printing this way was profitable for Lawrence, but it wasn't without problems – other publishers took advantage of its notoriety and lack of copyright, producing their own pirated versions, while booksellers became increasingly reluctant to stock it, after a bookstore manager in Massachusetts was sentenced for four months in prison for having copies in his shop.

Meanwhile the book's scandalous reputation grew. Described as reeking with 'obscenity and lewdness' some church-goers feared that even the sight of the novel would cause immediate and irreversible corruption. Their outraged response upset Lawrence 'The hatred which my books have aroused comes back at me and gets me here,' he is reported to have said, pointing at his heart, months before his death in 1930. After his death an edition expurgated of any hint of naughtiness was published with the assurance on the jacket that the remaining text still 'suggests to the greatest possible extent the original's strength and vigour.'

When unexpurgated editions were finally published, obscenity trials were launched against the publishers. Painful trials in America (which centred on the post office's refusal to allow it in the mail) and the UK shortly afterwards, established that *Lady Chatterley's Lover* was actually less obscene than literature that had been published later, and legal editions came into the bookshops for the first time. However, the Japanese publisher was convicted for bringing out a translated version, while in China during the cultural revolution the book was banned and anyone caught possessing a copy could be imprisoned for life. As late as 1987, the Ministry of Culture were still suppressing copies of the book and allowing only prominent people to read it, providing they had received a certificate authorising them to do so for academic purposes.

ANIMAL SEED DISPERSAL – BY TERMINOLOGY

Eight ways that animals disperse seeds

Ectozoochory – when animals disperse seeds outside of their bodies – usually stuck to their coats.

Endozoochory – when animals disperse seeds inside their body – often by certain species of birds, who have no teeth and soft gizzards, so that the seed is able to survive when eaten.

Scatterhoarding – the hoarding of a small number of seeds by mice in many different places.

Larderhoarding – the hoarding of a large number of seeds by squirrels in one or two places.

Inhumation – the dispersal of seeds near the entrance of ants' nests where they are fertilised by body parts and faeces.

Myrmecochory – the dispersal of seeds by ants.

Seed rewards – these are rewards offered by plants to encourage animals to disperse their seeds – rewards include a fleshy pulp with sugar, starch and protein.

Fruit mimicry – when seeds pretend to be rich in foods by being highly coloured or patterned, so that they can be consumed, passed and expelled by animals.

ON THE GRAPEVINE

Under the sweet-peas I stood
And drew deep breaths. They smelt so good.
Then, with strange enchanted eyes,
I saw them change to butterflies.

Higher than the skylark sings
I saw their fluttering crimson wings
Leave their garden-trellis bare
And fly into the upper air.

Standing in an elfin trance
Through the clouds I saw them glance...
Then I stretched my hand up high
And touched them in the distant sky.

At once the coloured wings came back
From wandering in the Zodiac.
Under the sweet-peas I stood
And drew deep breaths. They smelt so good.

Alfred Noyes, *A Child's Vision*

BLOOMING PUZZLES

What runs around a garden, but does not move?
Answer on Page 153

CELEBRITY GARDENERS

Charlie Dimmock may be well known for her beautifully inventive water features on *Ground Force*, but she is even more famous for being television's best piece of garden totty. Famed for not wearing underwear, Charlie is an icon for bra-lessness and was indeed branded a 'bra-less slapper' by *Loaded*. Despite the fulsome praise, Charlie herself seems oblivious to the lure of her twin charms and far more concerned with plastic pond liners: 'I find it fairly difficult to think of myself as sexy. I've never been called that in my life before. At school, I was fat and pasty and known as "carrot top"'. Still, men seem pretty much convinced; AA Gill wrote in *The Sunday Times* that 'Charlie should have seed packet instructions tattooed on her bottom: Hardy annual, doesn't need much attention. Good in shady spot. Keep moist and tie to stiff post.'

In addition to *Ground Force*, Charlie has presented numerous other gardening programmes – including *Charlie's Wildlife Gardens* and *Charlie's Garden Army* and there has been a whole host of other, non-gardening related shows.

QUOTE UNQUOTE

One for the rock, one for the crow,
One to die and one to grow.
ANON

A WATERY HONEYMAN COTTAGE

In 1812, Percy Bysshe Shelley spent his honeymoon with his bride Harriet in a rural retreat called Nantgwyllt House situated in the Elan Valley, Wales. But a century ago the house and its little cottage garden was flooded in an attempt to provide Birmingham with 20,000 million gallons of water. Now water levels are shrinking in the reservoir, one of a network in the Elan Valley, and visitors are flocking to the site, where the walls have been exposed, to look on the poet's home before it rains again.

THE JOY OF BEING A TUMBLEWEED

*Last to tumble to the fence, it was Thomas Tumbleweed's turn
to buy the beer again.*

IN YOUR HONOUR

Some plants have been named after famous botanists. These honours were most often conferred posthumously, and strangely enough the plants named after the botanists were not always ones that they had discovered or cultivated, but other plants that just happened to be discovered after their death, which needed a name.

Flower	Named after
Buddleia	Adam Buddle (1660–1710), *English botanist*
Clarkia	William Clark (1770–1838), *US explorer*
Dahlia	Andreas Dahl (1751–1789), *Swedish botanist*
Forsythia	William Forsyth (1737–1804), *Scottish gardener*
Fuchsia	Leonhart Fuchs (1501–1566), *Bavarian botanist*
Lobelia	Matthias de L'Obel (1538–1616), *Dutch botanist*
Tradescantia	John Tradescant (d. 1638), *English gardener*
Wisteria	Caspar Wistar (1761–1818), *US botanist*

ON THE GRAPEVINE

The roses red upon my neighbour's vine
Are owned by him, but they are also mine.
His was the cost, and his the labour, too,
But mine as well as his the joy, their loveliness to view.

They bloom for me and are for me as fair
As for the man who gives them all his care.
Thus I am rich, because a good man grew
A rose-clad vine for all his neighbour's view.

I know from this that others plant for me,
And what they own, my joy may also be.
So why be selfish, when so much that's fine
Is grown for you, upon your neighbour's vine.
Abraham L Gruber, *My Neighbour's Roses*

QUOTE UNQUOTE

To get the best results you must talk to your vegetables.
PRINCE CHARLES, quoted in *The Observer* in 1986

GARDENING CELEBRITY TOP TEN

When readers of *Amateur Gardening Magazine* voted for Gardener of
the Millennium in February 2000, 70% of them chose Geoff
Hamilton as their all-time favourite. The top dozen, in order of
popularity were:

1. Geoff Hamilton
2. Alan Titchmarsh
3. Percy Thrower
4. DG Hessayon
5. Charlie Dimmock
6. The Bloom Family
7. Gertrude Jekyll
8. Prince Charles
9. Mr Middleton
10. Dr Ernest Henry Wilson
11 = Carol Klein
11 = Clay Jones

TULIP PERFECTION

In 1847, Dr WRG Hardy published a ground-breaking treatise titled 'On Perfection of Form in the Tulip'. He devised four rules to detect perfection in florists' tulips:

1. Every tulip, when in its greatest perfection, should be circular in its outline throughout; its depth should be equal to half its width across from the top, or highest point, of one petal to the tip of the other immediately opposite.

2. It should be composed of six petals, three inner and three outer, which should all be of the same height, and have such a form as will enable them to preserve this circular outline; their edges being even, stiff and smooth; and their surfaces free from inequality of every kind.

3. The breadth of the petals should be amply sufficient to prevent any interstices being seen between them, so long as the flower retains its freshness.

4. There should be exact uniformity between the outline of the cup, and the outline of the upper margin of the petal, which should form an arc or curve, whose radius is equal to half the diameter, or whole depth of the flower.

FANTASY GARDENS

In the late 1940s Edward James, an English traveller on his way to Mexico City stopped off for a rest in a forest just outside a monastery at Xilitla. Edward was apparently looking up at the sky, when a cloud of butterflies descended, blocking out the light of the sun. This inspired him to build a public garden in the middle of the forest, and the resulting gardens, Las Pozas, are a delicate fantasy of towering colonnades, impossibly elaborate fountains, doors that appear to be entrances but are actually exits and staircases that lead to the sky. This lost world fantasy has become quickly populated with colonising vines and epiphytes that are devouring the dreamy architecture and returning it slowly back to jungle. What was in James's mind when he designed all this? We can only gain a clue from an inscription on the wall of his house: 'My house has wings and at times, in the depths of the night, it sings...'

THE DESPICABLE FELINES

Britain's gardeners have declared war on cats. And with an estimated 300 million birds and mammals killed every year by Britain's eight million cats, it's not hard to understand why. According to the Mammal Society, who asked over 4,000 people which animals they liked most to visit their gardens, cats fared very badly, only just beating rats at the very bottom of the table.

The completed results of the survey, listed below, asked people to rate animals that appeared in the garden out of 10.

Hedgehog	9.4
Badger	8.8
Deer	8.5
Fox	8.0
Bat	7.4
Grey squirrel	6.3
Mouse	6.1
Vole	5.8
Rabbit	4.6
Mole	4.5
Cat	3.7
Rat	2.9

Devoted cat lovers who wonder why their precious felines are attracting such criticism should take steps to prevent their pets from killing animals. Putting a bell round their necks and more importantly, keeping them indoors at night and in the early morning will make a difference. If you want to prevent cats in your garden, one of the most environmentally friendly ways of discouraging felines is to spray orange juice around the fences. Cats have a particular aversion to this smell and will stay away from it. Be careful of any more permanent measures – one gardener who attempted to discourage cats with a wire grid attached to a 12 volt battery charger electrocuted a 10-month-old kitten. He ended up before the magistrate's court where he admitted causing unnecessary suffering to an animal with a device that could have caused injury to a child.

MRS JEKYLL AND MR ED

Architect Edwin Lutyens and garden designer Gertrude Jekyll first met in 1889 and launched a friendship on the back of a rhododendron conversation. Five years later she asked him to build a house to go with her garden, and a great partnership was born. They worked on 70 house and garden commissions together – he designed the hardscapes and vistas and she designed the plantings.

120 *Recorded depth, in metres, that the roots of a wild fig tree penetrated in Echo Caves, South Africa*

LOOFAH

Thought your loofah was fished out of the sea? Think again.
The loofah is actually a sponge gourd – the fruit of a vine,
native to Asia, which grows in most tropical climates. Related
to the cucumber family, loofahs can be eaten when young.
The mature fruit is covered with a tough green skin.
Underneath this is the spongy gourd.

FEED THE BIRDS

In the autumn and winter, it is a hard job for birds in the garden to
find enough food. There's less food in the garden, and less time to
find it because of the shorter daylight hours. Yet because farmers
harvest their crops more efficiently (leaving less pickings in the
field) and more quickly (leaving less ripe crops out for birds) birds
need more. If you want birds in your garden all year round make
sure you have some late fruit such as crab apples, cotoneaster or
pyracantha. Or, cook up these nutritious bird cakes:

> 8oz of solid white vegetable fat
> 1 cup of oatmeal
> 1 cup of chopped nuts
> 1 cup of flaked maize
> 1 cup of kibbled wheat
> 1 cup of mixed bird seed
> 1 cup of vine fruits chopped or 6 cups of ready-made
> wild bird seed mixture

Gently melt the fat in a large pan. Place the dry ingredients into a
large bowl and pour the fat over them. Stir the mixture until the fat
is really well mixed with the dry ingredients. You will need
sufficient fat to hold the dry ingredients together as the fat begins
to cool. With damp hands, pat the mixture into small cakes and
leave to set in a cool place.

ON THE GRAPEVINE

> I used to love my garden
> But now my love is dead
> For I found a bachelor's button
> In black-eyed Susan's bed

CP Sawyer

APPLES, YOU ROTTER?

Native to the Sumatran rainforests, the corpse flower has the dubious reputation of being not only the world's biggest (it can grow to six feet tall) but also the world's smelliest flower, with a smell that mimics that of rotting flesh in order to attract the carrion beetle that pollinates the flower. It is also a plant under threat in the wild, and attempts to propagate it in the laboratory have proved very difficult; not least because it can take up to 15 years to flower, and male and female parts do not mature at the same time (making self-pollination impossible). Fortunately, Huntingdon Botanical Gardens in California successfully created a technique to pollinate the plant using a bag of rotten apples in 2000. The rotten apples produced ethylene gas, which encouraged the flowers to ripen early and allowed the plants to self-pollinate.

FLOWER FAIRIES

One hundred and fifty poems and illustrations make up the *Flower Fairies* series. Created by the writer and illustrator Cicely Mary Barker, the first of the *Flower Fairies* was published in 1923 to great popular acclaim. Each poem was accompanied by a delightful painting of a fairy whose appearance closely resembled the parts of the flower the fairy was used to represent. According to Barker's fairy lore, a new flower fairy springs to life every time a seed is planted, but these six-inch tall shy and secretive creatures will only reveal themselves to those who truly believe in them. And appropriately, little children who don't follow the fairy code will never catch a sighting...

The Fairy Code

- Be cheerful
- Be polite
- Work hard
- Be honest
- Be kind
- Be neat
- Be friendly
- Be generous
- Keep secrets
- Be humourous

GARDEN MEMORIES

A small memorial garden has been created in the middle of Grosvenor Square to remember the 67 British victims of the September 11 terror attacks in New York. Designed with a wooden pergola, which is etched with the phrase 'Grief is the price we pay for love', the garden's plants are carefully chosen, with the US native tobacco plant included as a symbol of unity between the USA and the UK, rosemary for remembrance and ivy for fidelity.

This famous children's garden was built in 1974 by *Blue Peter*'s first gardener (and one of the first celebrity gardeners) Percy Thrower. Together with David Bellamy and the Greater London Ecology Unit, the garden was transformed from a patch of barren waste ground into a full urban garden with four ponds and a mini-woodland. Percy worked in the garden, showing kids all over the country how to make their own mini garden plots and asking them to persuade their parents into the garden centre for promotions like 'plant a tree in '73'.

Percy remained highly popular with viewers and just before he died, *Blue Peter* presenters visited him in his nursing home and played him a video of clips of his time in the show. They also presented Percy with a Gold Blue Peter Badge and Percy declared it was just as important to him as his MBE and the Victoria Medal of Honour he received from the Royal Horticultural Society.

After his death, viewers suggested that a memorial garden should be added to the *Blue Peter* garden, and it duly was: two pink rose bushes were named after him and two hardy fuchsias – Percy's favourites – were planted in his honour.

In 1983, the garden was badly vandalised. Beds were covered with black fuel oil, pots and urns were smashed and thrown into the pond, the sundial was broken in half and the remaining flowerbeds trampled until all the flowers were killed.

The news was broken to the children of the nation that afternoon by presenters Simon Groom, Janet Ellis and Peter Duncan. Cue Janet Ellis: 'It's very sad to think that a few people take such pleasure from harming their fellow human beings and from hurting animals as well.'

Percy Thrower was reportedly devastated by the news, saying of the vandals, 'they must be mentally ill'. *Blue Peter* launched a clean up operation to return the garden to its former glory with a new statue and a tree planted for the year 2000. Security was also stepped up to avoid any further destruction.

Who was responsible? The perpetrators have never been caught, but the mystery came a step closer to being solved in 2000, when England footballer Les Ferdinand admitting 'helping a few people over the wall'.

The BBC decided not to take any action over the revelation.

GNOMES ON FILM

In the French hit film *Amélie*, the heroine's father Raphael Poulain turns to his garden in sorrow after the death of his wife. He builds a miniature shrine around his garden gnome, then adorns it with shells, hostas, daisies and proud plaster ducks. To cure him of his melancholy and help him realise his ambition to travel, Amélie secretly takes the gnome – a chipper individual with a long white beard, rosy cheeks and a pointed red hat – and gives it to an air stewardess friend who takes him around the world. Periodically Amélie's father receives intriguing photographs of his gnome against a famous city backdrop. By the end of the film, Monsieur Poulain is so inspired by the travels of his gnome, he takes off on a trip of his own.

What did Monsieur Poulain's gnome see on his grand tour?

Monument Valley, Arizona
The Empire State Building and the Statue of Liberty, New York
Red Square, Moscow
The Acropolis, Athens
The Blue Mosque, Istanbul
The Sphinx, Cairo
Angkor Wat, Cambodia

ON THE GRAPEVINE

Just now the lilac is in bloom,
All before my little room;
And in my flower-beds, I think,
Smile the carnation and the pink;
And down the borders, well I know,
The poppy and the pansy blow...
Oh! there the chestnuts, summer through,
Beside the river make for you
A tunnel of green gloom, and sleep
Deeply above; and green and deep
The stream mysterious glides beneath,
Green as a dream and deep as death.
– Oh, damn! I know it! and I know
How the May fields all golden show,
And when the day is young and sweet,
Gild gloriously the bare feet
That run to bathe...

Rupert Brook, *The Old Vicarage, Grantchester*

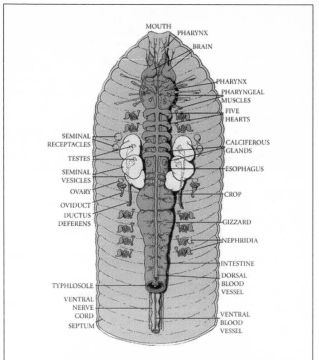

MOUTH
PHARYNX
BRAIN
PHARYNX
PHARYNGEAL MUSCLES
FIVE HEARTS
SEMINAL RECEPTACLES
CALCIFEROUS GLANDS
TESTES
SEMINAL VESICLES
ESOPHAGUS
OVARY
CROP
OVIDUCT
DUCTUS DEFERENS
GIZZARD
NEPHRIDIA
INTESTINE
DORSAL BLOOD VESSEL
TYPHLOSOLE
VENTRAL NERVE CORD
SEPTUM
VENTRAL BLOOD VESSEL

The inner workings of an earthworm showing male and female organs, five hearts and a stomach for earth grinding.

BEAR GARDENS

A 'bear garden' is an allusion for a noisy disorderly place. Bear gardens were popular public gardens where animal-baiting contests took place. During the reign of Richard II, Robert de Paris kept a bear garden on the bank of the River Thames. Christopher Preston established a bear garden in Hockley-in-the-Hole near Clerkenwell Green during the reign of Charles II where bear, bull and dog-baiting events were staged along with cock fights. Preston was famous for his gruelling bear fights but he received his come-uppance when he was killed by one of his own bears in 1709.

Age, in millions of years, of the oldest flowering plant, 125
Archaefructus sinensis *found in a fossil in China in 2002*

A DEEPER MEANING

Flowers in wedding bouquets are frequently chosen for their symbolism as well as colour and fragrance. A bouquet of daisies, ivy and lily represents innocence, fidelity and purity, while roses and orange blossom denote passionate love and fertility.

Name	Namesake
Bluebells	consistency
Blue violets	faithfulness
Carnations	distinction
Daisy	innocence
Forget-me-not	true love
Gardenia	joy
Ivy	fidelity
Lily	purity
Lily-of-the-valley	happiness
Magnolia	dignity
Myrtle	consistency
Laurel leaves	virtue
Orange blossom	fertility and happiness
Orchid	beauty
Red rose	passionate love
White rose	purity
Red and white roses	unity
Rosemary	commitment and fidelity

BLOOMING PUZZLES

A lavender bush is growing in a pot, and some bees are hovering over it. How many flowers and bees are there if, when each bee lands on a flower, there's one bee left over and when two bees land on each flower, there's one flower left over?

Answer on page 153

PLANTS AND SEX AND ROCK AND ROLL

For a while, cotton seed oil was used as a cooking oil in China in the 1930s, but it was thrown out of the woks when families who ate it discovered it had an unusual side-effect – as a male contraceptive! In fact, in all the areas where it was eaten, the fertility rate dropped alarmingly. The compound responsible for this is gossypol – and it's a very effective drug indeed. Following the discovery scientists made attempts to develop it into a male contraceptive. This was abandoned because of the high incidence of infertility, but some scientists are still considering it as an alternative to vasectomy.

TOOTHBRUSH TALES

Although modern toothbrushes with nylon bristles are a western invention that dates back to the 1930s, the toothbrush story goes as far back as 5,000 years, when Egyptians used small tree branches with frayed ends to ensure their dental hygiene. Europe imported the idea in the 15th century from China, where locals were using the neck hair of Siberian wild boar mounted on bamboo handles. But for centuries people have used parts of plants to clean their teeth – and still do. In East Africa, sticks from the *Diospyros* tree are popular natural toothbrushes, and have recently been found to contain anti-fungal properties. In the Middle East and India, the sticks of a tree unsurprisingly known as the toothbrush tree are chewed for their juice, which has been found to contain an anti-bacterial compound. And in Burma, locals chew a mixture of charcoal and salt – which apparently makes the teeth very white!

QUOTE UNQUOTE

The best place to find God is in a garden. You can dig for him there.
GEORGE BERNARD SHAW, playwright

PLANT PANACEA

In 2003, the BBC ran a poll to discover the nation's favourite novels. Several of the titles that made the final cut sound like gardening classics. The books, in their final positions, were:

5. *Harry Potter and the Goblet of Fire*, JK Rowling
13. *Birdsong*, Sebastian Faulks
15. *The Catcher in the Rye*, JD Salinger
16. *The Wind in the Willows*, Kenneth Grahame
22. *Harry Potter and the Philosopher's Stone*, JK Rowling
23. *Harry Potter and the Chamber of Secrets*, JK Rowling
24. *Harry Potter and the Prisoner of Azkaban*, JK Rowling
41. *Anne Of Green Gables*, LM Montgomery
51. *The Secret Garden*, Frances Hodgson Burnett
70. *Lord of the Flies*, William Golding
108. *The Wasp Factory*, Iain Banks
120. *The Day Of The Triffids*, John Wyndham
121. *Lola Rose*, Jacqueline Wilson
124. *House Of Leaves*, Mark Z Danielewski
145. *James And The Giant Peach*, Roald Dahl
157. *One Flew Over The Cuckoo's Nest*, Ken Kesey
172. *They Used To Play On Grass*, Terry Venables and Gordon Williams
199. *The Very Hungry Caterpillar*, Eric Carle
200. *Flowers In The Attic*, Virginia Andrews

*The greatest service which can be rendered to any country
is to add a useful plant to its culture.*
THOMAS JEFFERSON, third president of the US

HEATING UP THE GREENHOUSE

British summers are getting hotter and hotter, and the English cottage garden is now under threat from the effects of global warming, according to a joint Royal Horticultural Society (RHS) and National Trust report. According to the report, our gardens are already suffering from global warming and within the next 50–80 years, we could start finding it difficult to maintain the healthy, green lawns England is known for. Concerning weather trends include fewer frosts, increased winter rainfall and flood risks, earlier springs, higher than average yearly temperatures, and hotter, drier summers with risks of drought.

These weather patterns could provide major challenges to gardeners seeking to maintain and preserve cold-climate plants. And, although the longer growing season would provide greater opportunities to grow exotic fruits, the water-logged winters might kill off many Mediterranean species which dislike excess water. The warmer weather may also enable garden pests to survive winters, allowing them to attack plants when they are at their most vulnerable.

The RHS recommends starting adjustments to gardens now by:
1. Making sure new plantings are drought-tolerant
2. Planting long-term shelter for the garden during stormier weather
3. Digging gravel and organic matter into soil to increase drainage
4. Building water collection and drainage measures into new landscaping and structures
5. Creating a garden pond to benefit wildlife during dry hot periods.
6. Avoiding planting in areas liable to flood
7. Making sure slopes are adequately planted to avoid erosion
8. Avoiding plants that suffer in wet weather or drought
9. Avoiding removing long established trees and shrubs whose root systems can survive drought

GARDEN GAGS

What do you get if you divide the circumference of a pumpkin
by its diameter?
Pumpkin pi

FLOWER NATIONS

Six national flowers that originated in the country they represent...

Country	Flower
Bermuda	Blue-eyed grass
Dominica	Bwa kwaib (or Carib tree)
Madagascar	Flame tree
Malta	Maltese centaury
Seychelles	Tropicbird orchid
Singapore	Vanda Miss Joaquim orchid

FLOWER NATIONALISATIONS

...six national flowers that didn't originate in the country they represent...

Country	Flower	Originated From
Canada	Maple leaf	Japan
Barbados	Dwarf flame tree	Madagascar
Hungary	Tulip	Turkey
Indonesia	Jasmine	Madagascar
South Korea	Rose of Sharon	Turkey
Ukraine	Sunflower	Ecuador

A ROSE BY ANY OTHER NAME

...and six countries that share the same national flower.

Bulgaria	Rose
Cyprus	Rose
England	Rose
Iran	Rose
Luxembourg	Rose
Slovakia	Rose

ON THE GRAPEVINE

Beneath these fruit-tree boughs that shed
Their snow-white blossoms on my head,
With brightest sunshine round me spread
Of spring's unclouded weather,
In this sequestered nook how sweet
To sit upon my orchard-seat!
And birds and flowers once more to greet,
My last year's friends together.

William Wordsworth, *The Green Linnet*

WHAT'S IN A NAME?

Augustus	noble
Arachnoideus	cobwebby
Foetidus	stinking
Flaccidus	feeble
Ignavus	slothful
Sleratus	wicked
Vulgaris	common
Physalis	bladder
Delphinium	dolphin
Digitalis	finger
Fritillaria	dice box
Gladiolus	little sword

QUOTE UNQUOTE

*Suburbia is where the developer bulldozes out the trees,
then names the streets after them.*
BILL VAUGHAN, author

CELEBRITY GARDENERS

These days, the UK's best-known celebrity gardener has to be **Alan Titchmarsh**. He has presented many garden shows including *Gardener's World, Ground Force, How to be a Gardener* and *Royal Gardeners*.

Bought up in Yorkshire, Alan announced to friends at the age of 10 that he was going to be the new Percy Thrower. After leaving school he started as an apprentice gardener, went to agricultural college and completed training at the Royal Botanic Gardens, Kew. He then became a horticultural journalist, writing for many gardening publications, such as *Amateur Gardening* and *Gardener's World*. A prolific writer, he has published more than 30 gardening books, including his very amusing autobiography *Trowel and Error*.

Although gardening is his main love, Alan has also presented *Points of View* and *Songs of Praise*.

An unlikely sex symbol with an engaging yet down-to-earth manner, Alan has become so well known that he has his own fan club and is on permanent show at Madame Tussauds. His statue is apparently so popular with the ladies that it has to be cleaned of lipstick marks twice a week.

THE WORLD'S FIRST MAZE

Mazes are believed to have been in existence for at least 4,000 years. For the first 3,000 years, they were built in the form of unicursal labyrinths, which consist of a single convoluted path, without junctions. These labyrinths were not meant to be puzzles, but were for ritual walking, running and celebratory processions.

Who doesn't know the story of the minotaur in the Cretan Labyrinth? The myth tells that Minos approached Poseidon, the Greek God of the sea, to ask for a sign that he, and not his brother Sarpidon, would become king. Poseidon agreed to send a white bull but stipulated that Minos should then sacrifice the bull in Poseidon's honour. But when the snow-white bull swam out of the sea, Minos decided to keep it and sacrificed one of his own bulls instead. When Poseidon discovered Minos's trickery, he flew into a rage and decided to punish the young king by causing his wife Pasiphae to fall in love with the bull. Pasiphae longed to satisfy her passion and asked Daedalus for help. Together they constructed a hollow wooden cow covered with cow-hide which was wheeled into the white bull's field with Pasiphae hidden inside.

The result of this strange consummation was the minotaur, who was born with the body of a man and the head of a bull. It was a fierce and violent creature that Minos secreted in a giant labyrinth underneath his palace. Every nine years, as a punishment for killing his treasured son Androgeus, Minos punished 14 Athenians by forcing them into the labyrinth where they were consumed by the minotaur. On the third sacrifice, Theseus volunteered to go into the labyrinth and slay the minotaur. Like all the best stories he was helped by the love of a good woman – in this case Minos's daughter Ariadne, who gave him a ball of thread allowing him to find his way out of the labyrinth after killing the minotaur.

A BUDDING CUTTER

Before the invention of lawnmowers, grass had to be cut with sharp scythes, slashing it quickly to achieve a cut rather than just ineffectually bending it. When engineer Edwin Beard Budding saw 50 men flailing with scythes on the lawns at Blenheim Palace, he had the idea of inventing a machine to cut the grass instead.

Inspired by nap-cutting machines with helical blades that were run over cloth to give it a flat finish, he designed, and in 1830 patented, the first machine which trapped grass between two blades. It was driven by cogs which in turn were driven by a large roller, which in turn was pushed by a relieved scythe-worker.

The first tropical orchid is believed to have been imported into England in 1731 by a cloth merchant who found the plant in the Bahamas and managed to get it to flower in England the following summer. Following his success, orchids quickly became highly prized plants for wealthy collectors – who had enough money to provide greenhouses for them. Celebrated as badges of wealth and worldliness, symbols of man's triumph over the wilderness, plant hunters quickly stepped up their search for these beautiful, yet puzzling flowers.

Throughout the 19th century, orchid hunters searched all over the world for rare varieties. Many battled through remote forests in search of their beautiful prize which could earn them a fortune. In 1901, eight hunters started out on an expedition to a thickly forested area in the Philippines. Months later only one returned – one had been eaten by a tiger, one had been drenched in oil and burned and the other five had vanished in the forest, never to be seen again.

The intense competition between orchid hunters and the unyielding pressures placed upon them by powerful plant importers added to their difficulties. Most hunters were heavily armed, and wouldn't be keen to talk about the plants they collected or where they were going – if they did it was guaranteed to be false information designed to send a rival off on a wild goose chase.

Large numbers of plants were needed to import back to England, since a great deal of them died along the way. And such was the demand that plant hunters weren't too fussy about where their plants came from. One hunter who discovered a new variety of orchid growing in a cemetery in New Guinea had all the graves dug up to collect the plants. Another located some important orchids growing on human remains in a New Guinea forest and sent them back to England still stuck to the ribs and shinbones. Shortly afterwards another orchid was auctioned off in London still attached to the human skull it had been discovered growing on.

Highly prized orchids were removed in their thousands. The plant hunters literally stripped forests of all they could find. Even trees were cut down so that orchids could be collected from their canopies – one expedition hunting in Columbia felled 4,000 trees to collect 10,000 orchids. Whole areas of forests in South America were denuded of orchids and have been orchidless since. Moreover, there are still some species that were discovered and stripped from the forest during this period – later dubbed 'orchidomania' – that have never been seen in the wild since.

FANTASY GARDENS

Tony Duquette started out as a designer of flamboyant window displays. Becoming quickly known as a maverick designer, he went on to design elaborate theatrical costumes, startling interiors and dreamy movie sets. In 1949, following several trips to Asia, Duquette, started a whimsical garden at Dawnridge in Beverley Hills, inspired by the twisting temples and ornate pagodas of Thailand and Indonesia. The result was an opulent homage to a fantasy Asian village, with dragons emerging from windows, balconies bursting with lush tropical plants and trees seeming to emerge from first floor roof gardens. Duquette died in 1999, but his fabulous garden lives on.

FINGER FLOWERS

In 1542, Leonhart Fuchs established the Latin name *digitalis* for the plant we now know as the foxglove. *Digitalis* means finger in Latin, and the plant was apparently named so because it was known in some parts of England as the finger-flower, whose petals resemble the fingers of a brightly-coloured glove whose ends had been snipped off.

But this plant's distinctively shaped flowers have also been called a variety of other names, each inspired by the image of little fingers, or little paws. The word foxglove itself is believed to have come from the term folk's glove, as the plant was thought to resemble the gloves of fairies. Some even knew it as fairy fingers, and in one particularly charming variation, it was known as fox fingers because it was thought the flowers were worn by foxes to keep the dew off their paws.

BLOOMING PUZZLES

One Sunday, Percy decided to take his dog Fido to the local gardens – five miles away. Percy walked slowly, his dog Fido, who'd dug a bone in the ornamental cabbages on their last visit, ran all the way there at a constant eight miles per hour. When he reached the cabbages, Fido retrieved his bone and ran back to Percy, at the same speed.

Fido continued to run forwards and backwards between Percy and the gardens at the same speed until Percy reached the gardens. If Percy walked a constant four miles per hour, how far did Fido run in total?
Answer on page 153

Elizabeth, as they drove along, watched for the first appearance of Pemberley Woods with some perturbation; and when at length they turned in at the lodge, her spirits were in a high flutter.

The park was very large, and contained great variety of ground. They entered it in one of its lowest points, and drove for some time through a beautiful wood, stretching over a wide extent.

Elizabeth's mind was too full for conversation, but she saw and admired every remarkable spot and point of view. They gradually ascended for half a mile, and then found themselves at the top of a considerable eminence, where the wood ceased, and the eye was instantly caught by Pemberley House, situated on the opposite side of a valley, into which the road, with some abruptness, wound. It was a large, handsome, stone building, standing well on rising ground, and backed by a ridge of high woody hills; – and in front, a stream of some natural importance was swelled into greater, but without any artificial appearance. Its banks were neither formal, nor falsely adorned. Elizabeth was delighted. She had never seen a place for which nature had done more, or where natural beauty had been so little counteracted by an awkward taste. They were all of them warm in their admiration; and at that moment she felt that to be mistress of Pemberley might be something!

Jane Austen, *Pride and Prejudice*

BLOOMING PUZZLES

Find the anagram
DEAR CAT STAIN
Answer on Page 153

WHAT'S BEEN BURIED IN YOUR GARDEN?

When she sold her West Wales house to Margaret and Paul Kiely in 2002, Barbara Vessey forgot to tell them that she had buried her husband Norman in the back garden in a legal home burial. 'I felt like there was no need to know' she told the BBC afterwards. 'It's just a body which is finished with. I didn't think of Norman being here.'

But Mrs Kiely didn't share Mrs Vessey's views. Horrified, she obtained a Home Office licence to have Mr Vessey exhumed and cremated. But her difficulties didn't end there – the digger couldn't find the body and eventually her son had to dig it up with his own garden shovel. Mrs Kiely said the experience was not one she was likely to forget.

*Bugs are not going to inherit the earth. They own it now. So we
might as well make peace with the landlord.*
THOMAS EISNER, ecologist

CHELSEA FLOWER SHOW – BY NUMBERS

1. The world's most renowned gardening show was first held in 1862
   at the RHS garden in Kensington. It then moved to Temple
   Gardens in Embankment until 1911, when it moved to its present
   11-acre site in the grounds of the Royal Hospital, Chelsea.

2. The show was cancelled in 1917 and 1918, delayed for a week in
   1926 because of the general strike, and cancelled again during
   World War II.

3. The numbers of tickets available are limited to 170,000, an
   estimated 10,000 of which are bought by visitors from overseas.

4. There are more than 20 large show gardens on display (for which
   exhibitors have been known to spend up to £20 million on
   getting their plants just right for the day), about 30 smaller
   gardens, 100 floral exhibitors and 600 exhibitors in total.

5. The main exhibition tent covers nearly 12,000 square metres,
   takes 20 men 19 days to put up and is the largest of its kind in
   the world.

6. The great sell-off, which takes place at 4.30pm on the last day is
   announced by the ringing of a bell and the sight of garden
   enthusiasts wrangling for a piece of their own.

7. An estimated 6,000 bottles of champagne, 18,000 glasses of
   Pimms, 5,000 lobsters, 28,000 rounds of sandwiches, 70,000 ice
   creams and an astonishing 300,000 cups of tea are consumed
   over the four-day period – many of which are subsequently
   washed down the 185 temporary toilets wheeled into place for
   the great event.

QUOTE UNQUOTE

Earth laughs in flowers.
RALPH WALDO EMERSON, poet

Number of species of bamboo, growing in the bamboo garden 135
at the Royal Botanical Gardens, Kew

WHAT'S THE SMALLEST PLOT OF LAND REQUIRED TO GROW A COMPLETE AND BALANCED DIET?

This was the question posed by John Jeavons, an American gardener with a passion for preserving goodness in the soil. In the 1970s, he devised a three-section mini-farm, dividing one section for food crops, one for compost crops and one for income-generation crops. His garden yielded at least twice as many (and sometimes 15 times as many) vegetables as the American national average and his experiment has been adopted by gardeners throughout the world.

PIPPINS AND SONS

Hundreds of apples belong to the illustrious Pippin family. Here's a sample:

Name	First Public Outing	Fruiterer
Allington Pippin	Shown to the Fruit Committee in 1889	W and J Brown of Stamford
Ballinora Pippin	Exhibited at the RHS in 1898	Messrs Harland and Sons
Ball's Pippin	Shown to RHS in 1920	Mr Allgrove of Langley
Beely Pippin	Sent to the RHS in 1929	Rev HLF Sculthorpe
Bowhill Pippin	Included in the 1929 National Fruit Trials	G Bunyard
Eccleston Pippin	Sent to the National Fruit Trials in 1925	Mr Barnes
Langley Pippin	RHS award of Garden Merit 1898	Messrs Veitch's nursery
Saltcote Pippin	Sent to the RHS in 1927	Mr Herbert Chapman
Venus Pippin	Sent to the RHS in 1899	Mr Godfrey of Exmouth
Wyken Pippin	Introduced to England from Holland in about 1720	Lord Craven

QUOTE UNQUOTE

A perfect summer day is when the sun is shining,
the breeze is blowing, the birds are singing,
and the lawn mower is broken.
JAMES DENT, humorist

FANTASY GARDENS

The Site of Reversible Destinies in Kyoto is a garden designed to confound. Created in 1971 by Japanese conceptual artist Shusaku Arakawa and American poet Madeleine Gins, this 'garden' is situated in a large bowl, with wonky paths threading through half-submerged kitchen units, overturned sofas and roof tiles. It is a garden which upsets perceptions, challenges preconceptions, and induces a fair amount of deconstruction along the way. So bizarre is it that accompanying instruction leaflets are handed out to visitors, inviting them to find 'identical moments' (hopefully they tell you how to recognise one) and embrace the inevitable falls they experience in the Elliptical Field. Did you expect anything less from a conceptual artist/poet combination?

RANDOM GARDENING DEFINITIONS

Green fingers ....Something everyone else seems to have plenty of
Perennial ....This year, possibly; next year, unlikely
Flower bed ....Anywhere a dozen or more seeds might land
Knee ....A device for finding rocks in your garden
Seed catalogue ....A work of fiction with fantasy photographs
Spade ....Highly efficient back-pain generator
Weed...............A good example of the 'Survival of the Fittest' theory

ON THE GRAPEVINE

The unpolitical and steady trees
Tufted about our country never care
What hourly crisis prickle in the air
They borrow their opinions from the breeze
Christopher Hassell, *Crisis*

NEGLECTING YOUR GARDEN?
GO STRAIGHT TO JAIL

Neglecting your garden may primarily be bad for your plants, but it can have further-reaching consequences. Scrap collector Graham Ellison neglected to tidy up the old newspapers, broken fencing, and building materials in his front garden, and when the neighbours complained he continued to let the rubbish pile up. Once Derby City Council realised sending letters was to have no effect on him, it sent workers instead, and Mr Ellis was left with a tidy bill and a four-month prison sentence.

Number of years the Indian mystic Shivapuri Baba lived 137
– ostensibly due to his diet of raw tree roots and tubers

A ROSE BY ANY OTHER SHAPE

Rose flower-heads come in a variety of shapes:

Flat – a flat open flower-head with single or semi-double petals

Cupped – an open flower-head with single or double petals that curve gently outwards

Pointed – an elegant pointed flower-head with a high closed centre surrounded by semi-double to fully double petals

Urn-shaped – a curved flower-head with semi-double to fully double petals that flatten out at the head

Rounded – a bowl-shaped flower-head of double or fully double overlapping petals

Rosette – a bowl-shaped flower-head with double or fully double petals overlapping tightly

Quartered rosette – a flat shaped flower-head with double or fully double petals overlapping in a quartered pattern

Pompon – a small round flower-head crammed with small double or fully double petals

TULIPOMANIA

It seems scarcely credible in the 21st century, when tulip varieties are widely available, and cheap to buy, but between 1634 and 1637, there was such a demand for tulips in Holland that a single bulb of the Admiral van Enkhuisjen variety could sell for 5,400 guilders – the equivalent of 15 years' wages for a bricklayer from Amsterdam. During these three years, a period of intense speculation, known as 'tulipomania', gripped Holland's mercantile community as they fought to acquire the garden's greatest status symbol.

Economists and historians still puzzle over the boom that set the cost of a single bulb higher than a town house in the best quarter of Amsterdam. But, the flower's rarity, its intriguing capacity to 'break' and emerge in a different colour (which is now known to be caused by a virus spread by aphids), the rich alluvial soil around Haarlem in which tulips flourished, and Holland's emerging role in world trade are cited as reasons for the flower's astonishing emergence as a valuable commodity.

Speculators, middlemen and lawyers helped push the price of bulbs into the stratosphere, but rather like the dotcom boom of the nineties, the prices of tulips collapsed in 1637 when it was realised that gardeners and planters could no longer afford to buy or plant them.

138 *Number of species whose tallest specimens are on display at the Royal Botanical Gardens, Kew*

Gardening during the war provided special challenges. The blockade of Britain and food rationing saw to it that fresh fruit and vegetables were in very short supply. The more food a family could produce the better they could eat, and as a result, Britain's population readily tore up their ornamental beds, herbaceous borders and neatly cared-for lawns to grow fruit and vegetables.

The following extract, from Stephen Cheveley's *A Garden goes to War*, published in 1940, shows just how far the national obsession with space and productivity reached:

'To keep a family of five with an adequate supply of green and root vegetables all the year, about 250 square yards of land are needed, assuming a decent soil. This takes no account of potatoes, and it would require about another 160-180 square yards to produce a year's supply. I know full well that many people could do it on less land, but we are not all blessed with such skill or good soil.

'The next thing to settle is how much land should be given to each crop, and here one can suggest only a very rough guide. It will mean doing a bit of calculation to fit in the areas to circumstances in your own garden. Let us assume the crops will be grown in rows five yards long, then you can alter the number of rows given below to meet your conditions. The width to be allowed between rows is shown, as this must also be taken into account in working out the space for each crop'.

Vegetable	Number of rows	Distance between rows
Cabbage, autumn and winter	4	2ft
Savoy cabbage	2	2ft
Brussels sprouts	8	2.5ft
Sprouting broccoli	4	2ft
Kale	4	2ft
Cauliflower	4	2.5ft
Carrots, early and main crop	8	12in
Beetroot	2	12in
Parsnips	3	15in
Turnips for tops	6	12in
Turnips and swedes for roots	3	12in
Early peas	2	2.5ft
Dwarf peas	2	2.5ft
Runner beans	2	8ft
French beans	4	2.5ft
Broad beans	3 (double)	2.5ft
Onions	10	1ft
Potatoes, early and main crop	40	2.5ft

The **Jardin des Plants** in Paris, France includes a hedge maze that was built in the 19th century and restored in 1990. Visitors who make it as far as its centre will find a summerhouse for resting and pendulum bell.

At the **Herrenhausen Gardens**, in Hannover, Germany there is an octagonal hedge maze with paths 500m long that lead to a central octagonal pavilion. Built in 1674, it was restored in 1936.

Built in the gardens of the **Marquis of Alfarras**, Barcelona, Spain there is a fragrant hedge maze with statues and fountains which was built in 1922 and is Spain's most well-known maze.

At **Soekershof**, South Africa, a giant hedge maze was opened to the public in December 2002. Covering a net surface of nearly 13,000 square metres, this maze is one of the largest in the world. It has two entry and exit points and (thankfully) numerous resting places along the way. Plants include the cacti that were believed to have orignally been used in the labyrinth at Knossos, where confusing passages were terrorised by the legendary Minotaur of Greek mythology.

Australia's oldest and most famous maze is at **Ashcombe Gardens** at Shoreham in Victoria. With paths of over one kilometre long, it also includes a stunning circular rose maze that is constructed with more than 1,200 rose bushes, all of which have been chosen for their colours and perfumes. Flowering begins in October, and continues right through Australia's summer, until May.

In **Kowloon Park**, Hong Kong, there is a hedge maze situated in the beautiful and extensive Chinese gardens that were built on the site of a former military camp.

QUOTE UNQUOTE

He who plants a tree plants a hope.
LUCY LARCOM, poet

I GOT YOU BABE

The tiny *Wolffia microscopia* flowering plant can produce daughter plants very speedily, every 30–36 hours.
In fact one *wolffia microscopia* could be responsible for producing one nonillion plants (1,000,000,000,000,000,000,000,000,000,000) in just four months.

GENTLEMEN AT LEISURE

*It is a truth universally acknowledged that a single man
in possession of a good fortune must be in want of a lawnmower.*

QUOTE UNQUOTE

The love of gardening is a seed once sown that never dies.
GERTRUDE JEKYLL, garden designer

THROWING MONEY OVER THE GARDEN FENCE

Brothers Derek and George Alderson spent more than £25,000
between them fighting each other over a dispute about a piece of land
measuring just 60ft by 30ft.

Malcolm and Marlene Girling cut down a hedge in breach of a court
injunction and were jailed for 28 days and fined £8,000 during a
boundary dispute with their neighbours.

27-year-old Samantha Richards spent six weeks in jail over a fence that
was erected on a neighbour's property. The battle, which one judge
described as a 'tragedy of Greek proportions' has been raging for years
and already cost £100,000 in legal fees.

A GAME OF GARDEN I-SPY

In 1979, the Royal Society for the Protection of Birds (RSPB) asked its junior members to count the number of birds they saw in their garden. It was a simple request – to sit in their gardens for an hour during a specific weekend and write down how many birds they saw. Over the weekend large numbers of birds were 'watched' and the event proved very successful. Now known as Big Garden Bird Watch, the event is held on an annual basis and in 2001 it was opened to anyone, whether a member of the RSPB or not. That year 55,000 took part, many of whom filed their counts on the RSPB's website. In 2003, more than 314,000 people spent an hour in their garden watching local birds, and an incredible 4.5 million birds were seen from 101 species.

Over time Big Garden Bird Watch has provided a very good indicator of the decline of some bird species in the UK. The table below shows the average increase and decrease in garden birds since the survey first started.

	Average number per garden		
Species	1979	2003	% change
Starling	15	4.9	-67.4%
House sparrow	10	4.8	-51.5%
Blue tit	2.4	3.1	+27.6%
Blackbird	4	2.7	-31.9%
Chaffinch	3	2.2	-27%
Greenfinch	1	1.9	+87%
Collared dove	0.3	1.7	+502%
Great tit	0.9	1.5	+62%
Robin	2	1.4	-31.7%
Woodpigeon	0.2	1.3	+562.2%

GARDENERS AT CHATSWORTH

By 1900, more than 55 gardeners were employed in the famous gardens of the Duke of Devonshire at Chatsworth. Rank and file gardeners at Chatsworth wore cloth caps and earned about 10 shillings a week, while foremen wore bowler hats and earned about £40 per year.

BLOOMING PUZZLES

Unravel the following: KGGO
Answer on page 153

142 *Number of years ago that the Chelsea Flower Show was first held at the RHS garden in Kensington*

CHECK BEFORE YOU CHOP

Local authorities can protect a tree or group of trees or even a woodland by making a tree preservation order which prohibits felling, topping, lopping, up-rooting or any other wilful damage to a listed tree.

Trees which make a significant impact on their local surroundings are most likely to be protected. These can include hedgerow trees, but not hedges, bushes or shrubs.

Wilful cutters who chop down a tree protected by a preservation order may find themselves on the wrong end of enforcement proceedings in a magistrate's court. The court has powers to impose a fine of up to £20,000 and also order the replanting of the tree.

To make a Tree Preservation Order local authorities are required to give the land owner written notice and advertise the proposed order in the local newspaper. Objectors have 28 days to make their feelings known in writing.

Once an order is made, only the local authority can enforce it. A concerned member of the public can apply to the local authority for a protection order as soon as they are aware a tree is at risk, but they cannot take action on their own behalf.

CELEBRITY GARDENERS

Monty Don is the serious minded organic gardener who is the main presenter of *Gardeners' World*. He came to fame along with Richard and Judy as *This Morning*'s expert on gardening and has presented many other gardening programmes for Channel 4, including *Real Gardens, Fork to Fork, Lost Gardens* and *Don Roaming*. He has published many books and writes a gardening column in *The Observer*. Monty has very strong ideas on how to garden – he hates the idea of pouring chemicals into the ground and whole-heartedly endorses organic produce. As much at home in his own garden as on the television he enjoys the therapeutic benefits of gardening, once saying: 'Nothing heals me more than gardening'. Described as straight-forward and unpatronising, his good looks combined with a practical, earthy yet sensitive personality has ensured many female fans.

QUOTE UNQUOTE

The garden that is finished is dead.
HE BATES, author

SO THEY SAY

To be a pig in clover is to be in a comfortable situation
To hear the grass grow is to have acute hearing
To be a reed shaken by the wind is to be someone whose opinion is frequently and easily swayed
To say a tree is known by its fruit means you can judge someone by their actions
To bark up the wrong tree is to blame the wrong person
To rest on one's laurels is to be content with past achievements and not look to something new
To beat about the bush is to delay an action or a decision
To hide one's light under a bushel is to be modest and unassuming
To be caught in a cleft stick is to be forced between two difficult choices
To get the dirty end of the stick is to be treated unfairly
To take a leaf out of someone's book is to follow someone else's example
To have ants in your pants is to be restless

ON THE GRAPEVINE

The little fires that Nature lights –
The scilla's lamp, the daffodil –
She quenches, when of stormy nights
Her anger whips the hill.

The fires she lifts against the cloud –
The irised bow, the burning tree –
She batters down with curses loud,
Nor cares that death should be.

The fire she kindles in the soul –
The poet's mood, the rebel's thought –
She cannot master, for their coal
In other mines is wrought

Joseph Campbell, *Fires*

DEVOTING TIME

A rosary is a string of beads that is used in many religions to assist the memory, steady a devotee's concentration and open up awareness of the inner world during devotions. Rosaries are believed to have originated in India, where they were made of kneaded rose petals.

GNOME GNOTES

Gnomes are thought to have been invented by the 16th century German physician Theophrastus Paracelsus. A maverick physician and alchemist, Paracelsus believed that gnomes were real beings that had occult knowledge of the earth. According to the folklore gnomes can live up to 400 years and prefer to greet fellow creatures by rubbing noses. They are supposed to bring luck and help with jobs around the house and garden, which is why many are modelled holding shovels, brooms and wheelbarrows.

But there's no getting away from the fact that while some garden owners love 'em, their neighbours just can't stand 'em.

IT'S NO JOAK

'Sudden oak death' is a fungal disease that is new to the UK, yet could potentially be devastating. Initially it struck redwood trees in California but in 2003, it reached oaks, horse chestnuts and native beech trees in Cornwall. The fungus, which is known as *Phytophthora ramorum*, has killed 80% of one oak species in the western US. It was first seen in viburnum trees in garden centres in the UK, and has spread to rhododendrons, camellia, lilac, kalmia, yew and witch hazel. It appears to be spread by rainwater – fungus from one tree splashes onto another, where it spreads in a ring round the trunk, causing the sap to ooze out and the tree to die. The disease is so new it is barely understood.

In an attempt to prevent the disease, many rhododendrons have been destroyed, including rhododendrons at the Lost Garden of Heligan, where some species are over 150 years old.

ILL MET BY SUNLIGHT

The following plants are all rashers or stingers that either sting when brushed against, or worse, react with sunlight to bring out a nasty rash. It is thought that plants have developed such irritating defences to prevent themselves from being hungrily devoured by passing animals.

Poison ivy • Primula
Hogweed • Giant hogweed
Rue • Stinging nettle

HISTORY OF MAZES

From their early origins in the myths of Greece and Rome, labyrinths continued to grow in popularity throughout Europe, during the Roman empire, labyrinth motifs was used in mosaic pavements. In Scandinavia over 600 stone labyrinths line the shores of the Baltic Sea – over half of them in Sweden. The reasons for them are not altogether clear although it is said that many were built by fishermen, who walked through them in the hope of a good catch and a safe return. In England, turf mazes are thought to have first been constructed during the Dark Ages by Nordic settlers. In Germany, turf mazes were built for ritual processions and used in ceremonies for young apprentices who reached adult life. In medieval France, pavement mazes with 13 rings of paths were laid in the stone floors of gothic cathedrals.

As formal gardens began to be established throughout Europe and enclosed for protection against the foraging of wild animals, puzzle hedge mazes began to appear in them. At first they were an amusement of kings and princes, and to start with were only found at the wealthiest palaces. It was a trend that was believed to have began during the Renaissance in Italy when gardens were recreated in the classical styles of Imperial Rome.

In the 19th century, wealth created by the industrial revolution provided the beginnings of a leisure industry, and hedge mazes were built in public parks for general amusement. But in the first half of the 20th century, many mazes were irretrievably lost as a result of neglect during the two world wars.

However, the increase in leisure travel and tourism since the 1970s has caused an upsurge in the amount of mazes throughout the world, and more are being built now than at any other time in history. In Britain, there are now more than 125 mazes open to the public. Hedge mazes are particularly popular, although indoor mazes made of marble, stained glass and mirrors are also gaining acceptance.

ON THE GRAPEVINE

O Blackbird! sing me something well:
While all the neighbours shoot thee round,
I keep smooth plats of fruitful ground,
Where thou may'st warble, eat and dwell.

Alfred Lord Tennyson, *The Blackbird*

HOW MANY SPOTS HAVE YOU GOT?

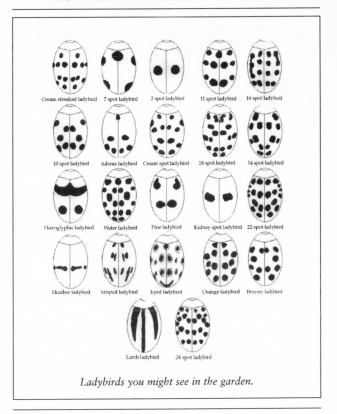

Ladybirds you might see in the garden.

AN ELDERLY SPECIMEN

The oldest tree in the world is believed to be a *Ficus religiosa* at Anuradhapura, thought to have been brought from India as a seedling in 288BC.

QUOTE UNQUOTE

Don't worry about the future; better laze under the trees, drinking wine and making fragrant our graying locks with roses.
HORACE, on the Romans' fondness for roses

BLOOMING PUZZLES

Homophones are words that sound the same but have different meanings. Find two homophones in the following sentence:
A tree by the sea
Answer on Page 153

QUOTE UNQUOTE

In Flanders fields the poppies blow
Between the crosses, row on row.
JOHN MCCRAE, soldier

NINE PLANTS FOR TRAVELLERS

Before the advent of the motor car, travel for ordinary folk was mainly on foot. Journeys were characterised by aching limbs, sore feet and long days out on the road. And to help travellers get over their long journeys, what better than plants to revive aching limbs, or speed them on their way?

Mugwort was believed to possess magical powers that prevented a traveller from becoming weary.

Germander speedwell was thought to speed journeys, and typically it was sewn into people's clothes at the outset of a long journey.

Prickly lettuce is also known as the traveller's compass plant because of its leaves' curious ability to twist themselves to face north and south – thereby directing anyone lost on the road.

Wild clematis commonly grew along the pathways and roads and was known as traveller's joy.

Leaves of **camomile** were inserted into the shoes of messengers in Ancient Greece in the belief that it prevented their legs from tiring.

The madonna lily, which is believed to have been bought to Britain by the Romans was squeezed onto the feet of Roman soldiers to cure their corns.

Lady's bedstraw was soaked in water and used to bathe sore feet.

Distilled water of hawthorn flowers was used to soak thorns and splinters out of weary feet.

A ROSY NIGHT OUT

The Romans believed that if they floated rose petals in their glasses of wine they would be immune from getting drunk.

DUTCH ELM DISEASE

Dutch elm disease is undeniably a part of the ecology of elms. The disease is complicated, relying on an extraordinary relationship between the fungus *Ceratocystis* and the elm bark beetle. First *Ceratocystis* attacks the tree and kills it. The newly dead tree attracts the female elm bark beetle, who excavates breeding tunnels into the bark and lays her eggs at the centre.

The grubs pass winter in the tunnels until the weather gets warmer, when they burrow their way out through the tunnels. At the end of the tunnel they pupate and turn into beetles, picking up the spores of the fungus on their bodies as they emerge. The grown-up elm bark beetle then flies off into adult life, first stopping off at another Dutch elm for a small bite...

The current epidemic of Dutch elm disease began in Gloucestershire in the mid 1960s. The disease spread very quickly – by 1983 it had killed every big common English elm in England, except in East Sussex. Overall, 20 million have been struck down.

Preventing the disease is very difficult – work in the past involved identifying and removing dying trees to prevent the bark beetle from excavating breeding tunnels. As the disease progresses – now in its third cycle since the 1960s, scientists are now looking at the possibility of altering the genes of either the tree, or the bark beetle to resist the fungus.

SO THEY SAY

To be as common as dirt is to be ordinary and unremarkable.
To feel as fresh as a daisy is to feel refreshed and clean.
To be led down the garden path is to be conned or influenced.
A bird in the hand is worth two in the bush is to be content
with what you've got.
To be as busy as a bee is to be well occupied.
To not see the wood for the trees is to fail to find the answer,
even if it is staring straight at you.
To be as cool as a cucumber is to be very laid back and relaxed.
To dig yourself into a hole is to put yourself into an embarrassing
situation by your own actions.
To have everything coming up roses is to have everything
going extremely well.
To sow your wild oats is to enjoy a period of sexual prowess.
To be a thorn in someone's side is to be a constant
annoyance to them.

FANTASY GARDENS

Nek Chand Saini was an Indian bureaucrat with a dream – to construct crowds of statues and herds of animals to populate a 40-acre public park in the city of Chandigarh – the 1950s style functional city designed by Le Corbusier. Nek Chand arrived in Chandigarh in the 1950s to inspect public works for the government and started to collect scrap from disused villages that had been cleared to make way for the new city. Secretly, on land set aside for conservation, he starting building statues, using techniques inspired by Le Corbusier's architecture – creating lost villages and fantasy kingdoms. Ten years later in 1975, officials stumbled across his extraordinary creations and insisted they had to be destroyed. But word of the statues quickly spread and hundreds of people started making their way through the forests to find Nek Chand's secret kingdom. Pressure on the authorities mounted, and they relented. The area was set up into a park and now more than 5,000 people continue to visit to see Nek Chand's famous figures.

ON THE GRAPEVINE

My neighbour... does the oddest things. She digs up clumps of violets from her outdoor garden and has them blooming exuberantly in pots, the small pink violet and the little almost-blue one, and as she takes the trouble to whitewash her pots, instead of leaving them to their normal hideous terra-cotta colour, you may imagine how the flowers gain in beauty as they pour over those blanced containers, white and clean as blancoed tennis-shoes. She digs up clumps of snowdrops and crocuses, and packs them into an ordinary pudding basin. One end of the house is all flowers and colour; the side-stagings are devoted to seed boxes.

She has not many real wooden seed boxes. There are cardboard dress-boxes tied round with string to prevent them from disintegrating, and old Golden Syrup tins, and even some of those tall tins that once contained Slug-death, and some of those little square chip-baskets called punnets. I verily believe that she would use an old shoe if it came handy. In this curious assortment of receptacles an equally curious assortment of seedlings are coming up, green as a lawn, prolific as mustard-and-cress on a child's bit of flannel. There are cabbages and lettuces in some of them; rare lilies in others; and I noted a terrified little crop of auriculas scurrying up, as though afraid that they might be late for a pricking-out into the warm earth of May.

Vita Sackville-West, *From In Your Garden*

DURING THE COMPILATION OF THIS BOOK, IN THE EDITOR'S GARDEN...

24 bulbs of elephant garlic were planted
of which 21 made a healthy showing

Seven new bags of leaf mould were stored behind the garden shed

A Cox's Orange Pippin produced nine treasured and
well-savoured apples for the first time in its life

35 tulip bulbs were planted of which six were eaten by
squirrels, five were given up on and the rest produced
beautiful white and purple flowers

One pineapple mint survived the winter but one pineapple sage
which was moved for the third time in two years didn't

The kerria rose which suffered from untimely pruning the previous
year recovered and burst into flower

One sturdy cat mint bought and planted out on 4 September
was discovered with just three sorry stumps remaining on
5 September after it was devoured by every cat in the
neighbourhood

Four orange – likely inedible – mushrooms appeared on the
Corylus stump

Six snowdrops made brief delicate appearances before the
first fall of snow

It snowed twice and rained too many times to count,
mainly on Saturdays and Sundays

Should I weed the lawn or say it's a garden?

Anon

BLOOMING PUZZLES

The answers. As if you needed them.

P16.   Leak and Leek

P19.   Cat's teeth – the rest are all plants.

P26.   They are all in space: *Pentas lanceolata* is star cluster; *Ipomoea
       alba* is moonflower; *Helianthus annuus* is sunflower

P35.   A sunflower

P42.   An icicle

P54.   Flour and flower

P64.   Pomologist – a cultivator of fruit

P70.   Owl

P74.   A robin's nest

P83.   Say it with flowers

P95.   A wheelbarrow

P100. Sixteen days. On the first day, the snail slithers five metres and
       slides back four metres at night, managing to get one metre
       nearer the lettuces. On the second day, he's therefore two metres
       closer, and so until after 15 days he's 15 metres closer. Then on
       the 16th day, he slithers to 20 metres.

P108. A mycologist studies mushrooms, a mycophile likes them, and
       a mycophagist likes to eat them.

P116. A hedge

P126. Four bees and three flowers

P133. As Fido was always running twice as fast as Percy, who
       travelled five miles, then Fido must have run 10 miles.

P134. Tradescantia

P142. Ginkgo

P148. Beech and Beach

Nothing is more the child of art than a garden.

Sir Walter Scott, poet and novelist

ACKNOWLEDGEMENTS

We gratefully acknowledge permission to reprint extracts of copyright material in this book from the following authors, publishers and executors:

Extract from *A Child's Vision* with kind permission from The Society of Authors as Literary Representative of the Estate of Alfred Noyes.

Extract from *The Tale of Johnny Town-Mouse* by Beatrix Potter, copyright © Frederick Warne & Co, 1918, reproduced by permission of Frederick Warne & Co.

Extract from *The Well-Tempered Garden* by Christopher Lloyd by kind permission of W & N Illustrated.

Extract from *Save Me The Waltz* by Zelda Fitzgerald by kind permission of David Higham Associates Ltd.

Extract from *One Perfect Rose* by Dorothy Parker reproduced by kind permission of Pollinger Limited and the proprietor. Originally published by Boni and Liveright.

Extract from *What is a Garden* from *Green Fingers* by Reginald Arkell, published by Herbert Jenkins. Used by permission of The Random House Group Limited.

Extract from *Hortus* by Nigel Colborn by kind permission of the author. Reproduced with permission of Curtis Brown Group Limited, London on behalf of the Estate of David Niven. Copyright © David Niven 1977.

Extract from *A Fragment of Truth* by Gael Turnbull by kind permission of the author.

Extract from *Gnomes and Gardens* by Alan Melville by kind permission of Maureen Hide.

Extract from *Through the Garden Gate* by Susan Hill by kind permission of Hamish Hamilton Ltd. Text copyright © 1986 by Susan Hill.

Extract from *Memoirs of a Geisha* by Arthur Golden published by Chatto & Windus. Used by permission of The Random House Group Limited.

Extract from *The Jewel in the Crown* by Paul Scott by kind permission of William Heineman.

Extract from *A Sense of Humus: A Bedside Book of Garden Humour* by Diana Anthony, published by Shoal Bay Press (1997), New Zealand.

Number of years it took for a specimen of a white cedar – the world's 155
slowest growing plant to reach the height of 10.2cm

Adams, Abby 56
Adams, Douglas 64
Adams, Richard 49
Allen, Woody 41
Anthony, Diana 15
Arnold, Matthew 19
Austen, Jane 75, 134
Bates, HE 143
Blake, William 74
Brook, Rupert 124
Budding, Edward Beard 14, 131
Bush, George W 16
Campbell, Joseph 144
Cannabis 89
Carroll, Lewis 104
Celebrities in the garden 71, 86, 105, 118
Climate and weather 13, 30, 37, 89, 92, 110, 128
Colborn, Nigel 31
Conan Doyle, Sir Arthur 76
Cowper, William 107
Creatures 21, 35, 49, 51, 54, 58, 63, 65, 66, 70, 84, 109, 120, 121, 125, 142, 147
Definitions 16, 36, 41, 60, 64, 72, 73, 77, 99, 103, 137
Dent, James 136
Dimmock, Charlie 116
Don, Monty 143
Dudley, John 99
Edible plants 22, 85
Eisner, Thomas 135
Emerson, Ralph Waldo 135
Endangered species 29, 60, 77
Erickson, Lou 35
Ernest, Shirley 113
Fantasy gardens 21, 57, 76, 97, 98, 104, 119, 133, 137

Fiction 11, 29, 100, 112, 114, 122, 127
Field, Ernest 17
Fitzgerald, F Scott 46,
Fitzgerald, Zelda 88
Flowers 33, 36, 85, 126, 129
Freud, Sigmund 46
Fruit 10, 31, 34, 70, 79, 93, 122, 136
Fungi 44-45, 74, 81, 95
Gandhi, Mahatma 21
Garden disasters 14, 66, 107, 134, 141
Garlic 106
Gaudi, Antoni 21
Gavin, Diarmuid 108
Glendinning, Victoria 112
Gnomes 17, 50, 70, 81, 82, 124, 145
Golden, Arthur 32
Grass 73, 80
Grenfell, Joyce 40
Gruber, Abraham L 118
Hamilton, Geoff 88
Harrison, George 40
Hassell, Christopher 137
Herbs 22, 50, 67, 87
Hill, Susan 87
Historic gardens 21, 51, 61, 97, 113, 125, 142
Horace 147
Inventions 10, 14, 131
Jarman, Derek 57
Jeavons, John 32, 136
Jefferson, Thomas 128
Jekyll, Gertrude 120, 141
Jerome, Jerome K 62
Kipling, Rudyard 69
Larcom, Lucy 140
Latin names 19, 26, 36, 110, 117, 130

Number of years ago, in 1848, that the first Miller's seedling apple was raised by James Miller in Berkshire

Lawrence, DH 114
Leaves 47, 109, 113
Legend and mythology 19, 20, 33, 89, 96, 113, 148
Legislation 15, 23, 55, 65, 79, 100, 134, 137, 141, 143
Linnaeus 27
Lloyd, Christopher 57
Lloyd, John 64
Love in gardens 20, 35, 71, 80, 91, 116, 126, 134
Mazes 42, 62, 63, 105, 131, 140, 146
McCrae, John 148
Medicinal plants 29, 42
Melville, Alan 25
Mistletoe 96
Moore, Clyde 28
Nash, Ogden 23
Natural oddities 28, 30, 50, 78, 94, 117, 122, 126, 140
Nichols, Beverley 19
Nicholson, Harold 26
Noyes, Alfred 115
Orchids 74, 81, 112, 132
Origins 16, 31-32, 41, 60, 92-93, 110, 129, 133
Parker, Dorothy 13
Pasternak, Boris 92
Paxton, Joseph 47, 52
Peat 83
Phobias 48, 90
Plato 12
Poisonous plants 12, 20, 25, 30, 34, 44-45, 52, 83
Potter, Beatrix 48
Practical gardens 15, 18
Proverbs and Sayings 57, 70-71, 80, 91, 96, 144, 149
Puzzles and gags 16, 19, 23, 28, 34, 42, 54, 64, 70, 74, 80, 83, 95, 100, 108, 116,

126, 128, 133, 134, 142, 148
Rogers, Will 53
Roses 33, 52, 74, 129, 138, 144, 148
Royalty 14, 15, 16, 29, 34, 37, 64, 72, 74, 91, 96, 111
Sackville-West, Vita 150
Saints 69
Scott, Paul 94
Seeds 36, 53, 54, 81, 84, 90, 103, 115
Shakespeare, William 20, 58, 67, 79, 99
Shaw, George Bernard 127
Singer Sargent, John 99
Societies 17, 26, 35, 45, 128, 135
Socrates 12
Sundials 82
Tennyson, Alfred Lord 39, 146
Thrower, Percy 73
Tips and advice 23, 29, 32, 53, 87, 94, 98, 107
Titchmarsh, Alan 130
Tools and accessories 18, 24, 43, 57, 62, 141
Trees 14, 21, 77, 103, 108, 110, 143, 145, 147, 149
Turnbull, Gael 52
Uses 11, 26, 29, 69, 121, 127
Vaughan, Bill 130
Vegetables 33, 55, 58, 95, 101, 106
Verdi, Giuseppe 24
Von Arnim, Elizabeth 92
Ward, Nathaniel 43
Watt, James G 80
Weeds 33, 56, 85
Wellington, Duke of 52
Wilde, Kim 48
Wordsworth, William 129

Cost, in pounds, of a six-month part-time RHS General Examination in 157
Horticulture course at the London School of Horticulture and Gardening

FOR YOUR GARDEN NOTES

Average number of days of the year that gardens are frost-free in Logan, Utah

THE COOK'S COMPANION

Whether your taste is for foie gras or fry-ups, this tasty compilation of the wise, the weird and the faintly absurd will soon have you asking for more. *The Cook's Companion* is an essential ingredient in any kitchen, and is boiling over with foodie facts, fiction, science, history and trivia.
160pp. 2004. ISBN 1-86105-772-5

THE TRAVELLER'S COMPANION

For anyone who's ever stared at a distant plane, wondered where it's going, and spent the rest of the day dreaming of faraway lands and ignoring everything and everyone else. Discover the world from your armchair as you dip into the history and mystery of international travel.
160pp. 2004. ISBN 1-86105-773-3

THE WILDLIFE COMPANION

For anyone who ever heard a bird sing, watched a moth flutter against the light, or ambled through a bluebell wood, and wondered, just momentarily, how such a diverse and beautiful natural world could possibly have come about.
160pp. 2004. ISBN 1-86105-770-9

AND COMING SOON...

THE LITERARY COMPANION 1-86105-798-9

THE LONDON COMPANION 1-86105-799-7

THE MOVIE-GOER'S COMPANION 1-86105-797-0

THE POLITICS COMPANION 1-86105-796-2